Lessons From My Son's Tattoo

Lessons From My Son's Tattoo

Living With Resilience, Despite the Unthinkable

Caryn Franca

ISBN: 1545300542
ISBN 13: 9781545300541
Library of Congress Control Number: 2017905662
CreateSpace Independent Publishing Platform
North Charleston, South Carolina

Table of Contents

Preface

I see the reflection of our family in the storefront glass and think, *Is this really us?*

It's Thanksgiving in picture-perfect small-town America. A seemingly ordinary looking family piles out of a minivan and a car. Mom and dad walk beside their daughter and her husband, with a baby on a hip and a toddler in tow. They walk as a family, with adult children, grandchildren, and a teenage son. They step through the glass doors into a shop.

...and that shop is a tattoo parlor, and yes, that family is really us.

I know if I saw something like that, I'd probably stop and stare. Was there a camera crew hidden, shooting the scene for a TV show? Did some crazy rock star's family move to town? Was this their special Turkey Day tradition?

No, Not exactly.

The family walking into the shop was mine. Our reason for getting inked as a family was, unfortunately, not exactly whimsical. Sixteen months before, our youngest son Nick, had begun his six-year battle against a rare and deadly form of cancer. That November, second Thanksgiving since his diagnosis, he designed a tattoo to commemorate his battle. Since our whole family had all been battling right alongside him, he wanted each of us to mark the journey too—by getting our own version of his tattoo inked, somewhere on our own flesh.

Nick put a lot of thought into the design of his tattoo. He created a four-point compass, with the words "Family," "Friends," "Strength," and "Courage" at the points, and "Faith" inscribed at the center. Those five words had been, and would remain, his guideposts as he battled, traveling a path no child should ever have to walk—one he faced with grace, dignity, and humor.

This is his story.

This is our story.

Why this book? Why am I sharing this story now? I've had a few years to heal. Why have I turned back to the journals I kept over those long, difficult years? Why do I choose to relive the pain and the horror? What is my purpose? What do I hope to accomplish?

Honestly, I write this book because I have to.

When Nick was sick, and in the years since, friends and strangers who read my journal entries faithfully told me I gave a voice to feelings and thoughts that they couldn't express. This book is my hands and my heart, reaching to connect to humanity by sharing my experience. It is a voice for those who suffer in silence without support. It is a tool for those who are paralyzed with fear to know they aren't alone.

There are self-help books that give concrete steps on how to change, grow, prosper, accept, and survive. This book isn't a step-by-step guide on how to live through trauma and loss. Those lessons are demonstrated anecdotally, through our story. This book reveals many *lessons (some will be in italics as you read)* I discovered during the hardest time of my life. It promises that the darkness that blinds us in life will slowly lift and that light will shine through and heal the cracks of our brokenness.

That's what Nick and his tattoo taught me. I hope it teaches you too.

Introduction

Like any victim of war, or abuse, or trauma, I have flashbacks.

They come with the intensity and regularity of a contracting womb. Painful images push and pull deep inside me, bringing a pain so instant and so intense that tears drip without warning. A day does not pass without the familiar ache swelling in my heart, always catching me off guard.

My womb opened to allow my son Nick to take his first breath, but my heart broke when he took his last.

But this is not a book about the way my beautiful boy died; it is about the amazing way he lived. When the unthinkable happens, the choice becomes one of survival or surrender. At the age of fifteen, Nick chose not only to survive, but to really *live,* and grow, and learn. Throughout those six unbearable, beautiful years, he inspired everyone around him to do the same. The words he had tattooed on the compass on his back, and are now etched on the marker above where his ashes are buried—"Courage," "Strength," "Friends," "Family," and "Faith"—were his creed. They were the words he chose to help him navigate the surreal life he lived for six years. They are the words that still guide me today.

Courage

As a mom, wasn't I the one to teach my son how to be brave? It ended up being quite the opposite. Surrendering control over fear that sears your heart is not easy. Learning to accept, to give grace to yourself, to move through the fog of an uncertain path—all this took a courage I didn't understand. I watched my fifteen-year-old and learned from his innocent acceptance. You see, sometimes the innocence of youth opens our eyes to possibilities that we were blinded to. As you read our story, you will witness countless situations where courage was called upon. You'll see us stumble, but you'll see us rise. You'll learn with us, to take those situations in your life that seem impossible and reframe them. Outcomes are unpredictable. We want to control our lives, and we certainly want to protect our loved ones from unthinkable situations. That's just not life. Life is hard. Life is outrageously unfair. Life takes courage. Take inspiration from us, into your own life. Tap into the hiding places of your soul when you have to navigate challenges that ask you to be braver than you think possible, and find courage to carry on. Find courage to set small goals and to not look too far ahead.

Strength

If you haven't been challenged in your life to carry a burden that requires a heavy emotional load, you will. We don't walk on this earth for decades without tragedy finding us. Death, divorce, abandonment, addiction, betrayal—the list goes on. These are the ugly bumps on the road of our humanness. These are the times when we are called upon to be strong, to forgive, to turn the other cheek, to persevere. How do we do this? Our six-year battle with our son who defied all odds taught us an inner strength that grew into a resilient attitude. I got so tired of people telling us how strong we were. We just learned to cope and to march forward with fortitude. We didn't feel strong most of the time. That's the lesson. What we see on the outside of someone's life rarely matches what may be raging inside of them. The internal fortitude to cope, manage yourself, and support your loved ones during crisis is what strength is. We've got it inside of us, but we just don't know it until we are asked to flex our emotional muscles. Through his story, my son may inspire you to walk through life's challenges with a new sense of strength. He became a master of setting small goals, and working towards them with every ounce of strength he had.

Friends

Children make friends simply and with ease. As we grow older we are more guarded, less open, and more likely to hold back from having intimate friendships. I am here to tell you, be like a child! Cultivate friendships, no matter what your age. Create real, raw, supportive relationships that you can count on. Learn to show up, and learn to ask tough questions. The connection of friendship is one of the absolute strongest threads that can hold an unraveling life together. The value you place on building lasting friendships during all phases of your life will make a big difference in how you are supported when those dark bumps of humanness knock you off your feet. Think about who you are as a friend, and how you are received as a friend, as you read our story. There are lessons of friendship woven throughout. Gestures from friends made our impossible life seem not as lonely.

Family

What do you tell your family when life is falling apart? How much do you tell, who do you need to protect, and who do you lean on? Our modern world has many definitions of family. Often, it isn't even blood that makes family. Many people have broken families, lost relatives, and dysfunctional relationships. How in the world can family be a guidepost for survival and resilience? The simple answer is- they decide to let go of struggles and just show up, raw, messy and real. They realize that blood is thicker than drama. They come into the situation and become the glue. Whether you have a nuclear family that is intact and is supportive, or you have a family that is scattered and not close, family still matters. Make amends, reach out, and ask for help. Remember, it isn't up to you to control the answers; it is up to you to ask for support. How they respond is their issue, not yours. The lessons of family ring loud in this book. Reflect on who your family will be, if crisis happens. Whether by blood, or by friendship, always have a supportive, intimate team that can pull you along when you can't see your way.

Faith

When my son chose to put faith at the center of his tattoo, I was a bit surprised. We had our faith tested. We questioned prayer. We saw religions from around the world all represented in the hospital in New York, and we saw a lot of prayers not answered. We were pissed. We were cynical about the whole everything-happens-for-a-reason philosophy. Where was this God who was so loving, when we were suffering? We had prayer chains, prayer circles, vigils, and laying on of hands, and my son died. So how does faith really work? Through our journey, what I can say is that faith goes beyond a certain religion. Faith is a belief that if you keep breathing and keep moving, there will be little miracles that are revealed. They are small, unexplained things. It is the recognition that, despite not getting what you want, you get small affirmations that there is a spiritual realm that whispers, "Keep going- you aren't alone."

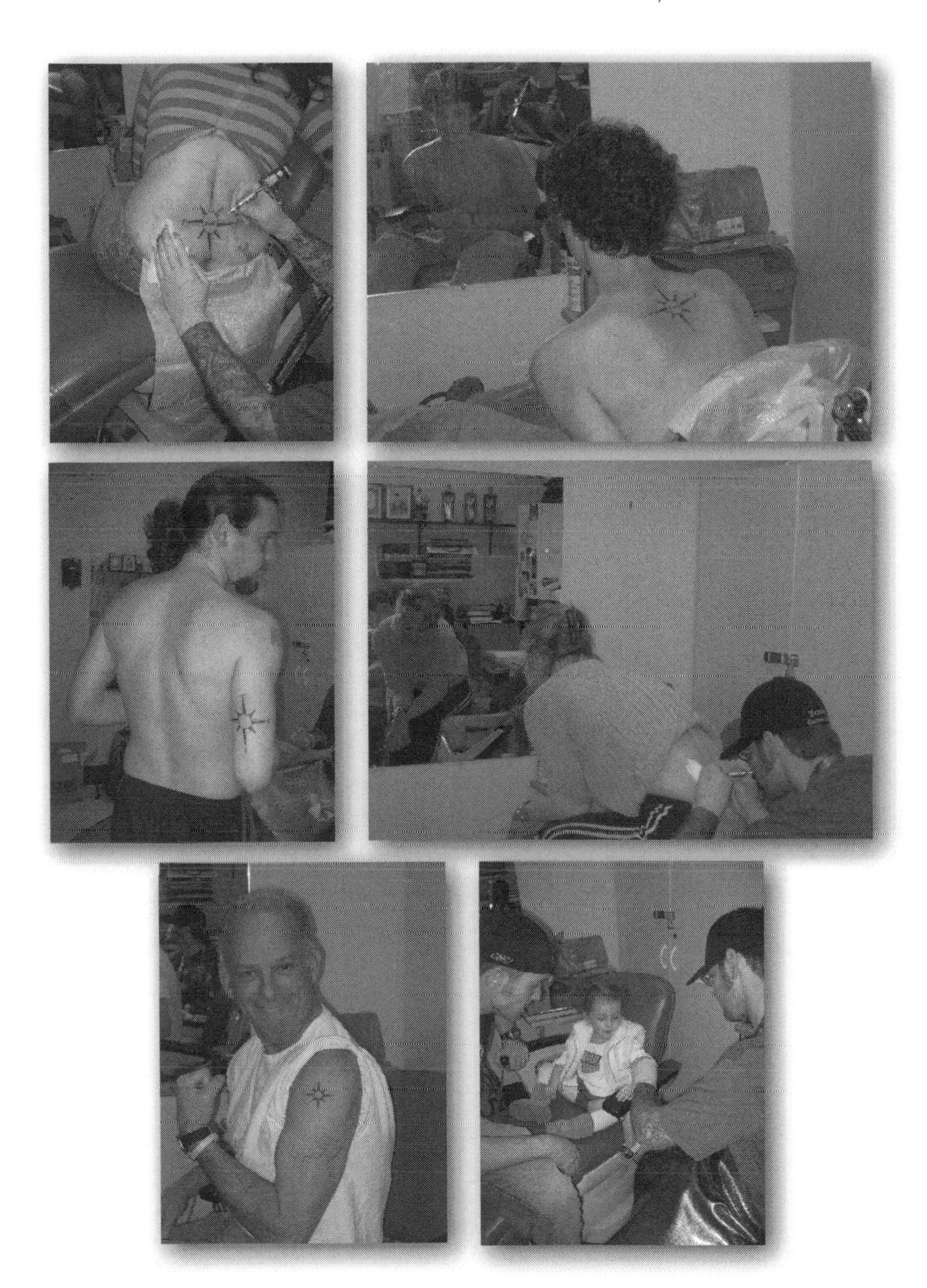

I

The Unthinkable- Summer2005

The Compass Point of Courage

Courage was something that had never really been tested in my life. Although I had seen it from afar and empathized with what others experienced, I never really knew what it took to live with courageous intention. My son taught me that over and over.

The Life We Knew

The spring of 2005 had been a blissful time. My children surprised my husband, Jim, and me with a beautiful twenty-fifth wedding anniversary celebration. We renewed our wedding vows with our children by our side, surrounded by a rock-solid circle of friends we had known for decades. Our youngest son, Nick, literally glowed that March night. His older sister, Alyson, and older brother, Jeff, had choreographed a reenactment of our wedding. Nick took the role of the minister, asking me to repeat after him as I pledged my commitment to our marriage.

I will always remember that as a perfect moment in our lives.

The conversations we were having that spring had seemed so important. When would we do our addition? Should I start conducting seminars? Would Jim move his office home? Could we afford to take the whole family to Jamaica for Christmas? How should we invest our money?

At just after midnight on June 14, those questions ceased to matter.

It was as if a giant bird scooped us up from the world we knew and dropped us down a dark and seemingly endless hole.

It began earlier that day, when I picked up Nick from school. He complained of pain in his upper-stomach area and came home and rested on the couch. This was not normal for him. The pain started moving to his right side, but I thought it was just gas or maybe nerves from exam week approaching. Jim was out of town, Nick didn't seem that bad, so I went to book club.

Shortly after I arrived at book club, Nick called. He was throwing up and the pain was worse on his right side. I rushed home in the middle of an enormous thunderstorm, a harbinger of things to come. I picked Nick up and drove him to our local urgent care center. They sent us straight to the emergency room with a diagnosis of appendicitis. It poured rain, and Nick moaned in horrible pain. I started to panic. I had never seen one of my children suffer like this—and I was scared.

They said the surgery would take about forty-five minutes. Two hours went by with no sign of the surgeon, and I was a nervous mess. My daughter, who had joined me at the hospital, told me I was overreacting. But deep inside me, I had the distinct feeling that something was very wrong. Call it mother's intuition. It was my first deep, intuitive awareness of that bird, circling over us, waiting to pluck us from the life we knew.

The doctor came out and said he had done a traditional surgery instead of utilizing a laparoscope. During surgery, he had discovered a bowel abnormality that he removed and he found a "small cyst" very near Nick's spine. He didn't think it was anything to worry about, and we went to visit Nick in recovery.

My mind kept wandering back to that word: "cyst." The surgeon told me it was probably just a congenital malformation and that Nick should have a CAT scan (Computed Tomography Scan) sometime over the summer, just to make sure. I couldn't help remembering a dear friend of mine, who took her own daughter to the hospital for appendicitis, only to learn she had something else: a hideous cancer called neuroblastoma. That cancer had taken my friend's daughter's young life several years before. I mentioned this to Jim. He told me I was blowing it out of proportion and that I should stop thinking negatively.

Knowing somehow that something felt dreadfully wrong, I went online. I desperately searched the internet for a logical reason why my perfectly healthy, normal fifteen-year-old had a cyst on his spine. No good answers appeared to ease my mind. After a few days, I finally worked up the nerve to type the word that was haunting me into the internet search box: "neuroblastoma."

One of the unusual—but possible—primary sites was the spine. I turned off the computer and vowed to try and think only positive thoughts from then on.

Spring gave way to summer, and less than two weeks post-surgery, we visited my parents to play in an annual golf tournament. Nick only had enough strength and stamina to play through sixteen holes before total fatigue took over. Shortly after that weekend, he departed for Camp Varsity, his beloved summer camp. We scheduled his CAT scan for when he returned home.

Beach Trips and Bad News—June 2005

Before this we had a vibrant, healthy family devoid of major sickness. Any sort of medical test was a big deal in our world. This scan was no exception. Nick complained when he had to drink chalky muck. He was angry and bothered at what seemed to be an inconvenience.

After the CAT scan, as the nurse technician walked toward me, that powerful motherly intuition struck again. She told me they took a few more pictures than they originally intended. Several days later, the call came that the CAT scan was inconclusive and an MRI (Magnetic Resonance Imaging) was necessary. This also was inconclusive. We were sent to a specialist.

That was the first time I heard the word "oncologist."

I froze with panic. Just the word meant death to me. What was an oncologist but a doctor who helped people die? How could they even think that my son needed to see an oncologist? We ended up having a PET (Positron Emission Tomography) scan ordered by our local hematology oncology children's group. They also wanted a more specific MRI done to the spinal area.

Still, through all of this, everyone we consulted assured us Nick was probably fine. The word "ganglioneuroma" was mentioned. Still everyone told us not to worry, as it looked to be benign. A needle biopsy was performed, and it came back benign. We were told the PET scan would hone in more on the actual activity and that could mean "abnormal cell activity." Those words made me nauseous. Abnormal cells couldn't be in my son's body.

While we waited for those results, we went on with our lives. We had plans to scoot down to the beach for a few days with a group of good friends, including two of Nick's best buddies. It was a seven-hour drive, so we were set to leave at four in the morning. The car was packed and the boys were sleeping in the basement. We expected the PET results after the weekend.

At eleven that fateful Friday night, the oncologist called. She said the results of the PET scan were not what we had all hoped for.

There were two hot spots in the scan and possible bone-marrow involvement. She wanted to schedule surgery as soon as possible. She told us bone-marrow biopsies would be performed while Nick was under anesthesia for the surgery.

I recall getting into the fetal position on my bed. I rocked back and forth, breathing hard, trying not to vomit. Jim kept asking, "What did she say?"

All I could say was, "The PET was positive."

How was I supposed to tell my unsuspecting, sleeping fifteen-year-old? Until now he thought his only problem was an inconvenient, yet benign tumor, that had to be removed. We decided to leave later and that we should tell Nick before we left. After a sleepless night, Jim and I explained to our son that the PET scan had "hot spots," and we needed to schedule surgery as soon as we returned.

The seven-hour drive to the beach was unusually quiet. The boys slept in the back most of the way. As I gazed at Nick in the rearview mirror, it seemed impossible to me. I curled up and silently let tears stream down my face as we drove down Route 95.

The next few days were surreal. All the normal beach activities were intertwined with cell-phone calls to doctors and calls from well-meaning friends offering love and support. I recall sitting on the beach with my friend drinking a glass of wine, watching the sun drop below the horizon. I looked at Nick and his two friends diving in the surf. They were chasing each other and laughing and knocking each other under the water.

I vividly recall thinking- this was the end of his innocence.

"Pancho" and Premonitions—July 2005

The next two weeks passed by in a blur. Nick had things to do. He tried out for the high-school golf team and went back to Camp Varsity for his last year as a camper. Both of those things seemed much more important to him than the interruptions he had to tolerate dealing with a cyst, which by this point he had nicknamed "Pancho."

The surgeon called and consulted with us while he was at camp. Surgery needed to happen immediately. That meant we had to call Nick. Parents don't call camp unless it's an emergency. When Nick was called to the phone, he knew the news was not good.

The surgery was major and extensive. It required that his spine be lifted off, replaced, and then his abdomen would be opened up. Two surgeons went to work on him, one after the other. We had been warned that the surgery could cause paralysis in the lower body affecting bowel, bladder, and sexual function. We all signed the consent forms and prayed.

The oncologist started with bone-marrow biopsies. The surgeons followed, and nine hours later both surgeons gave us the glowing news that the flash biopsies were benign and that the tumor did not have any traits that would indicate cancer. As Nick recovered in the intensive care unit, we cautiously rejoiced that this nightmare would soon be over.

When Nick woke up, he was every inch the fifteen-year-old boy. Still in a medicated stupor, he managed to ask, "Does my dick still work?" I told him it did, and by the way, his legs did too! After a day in intensive care, Nick was to be moved to a regular hospital room.

But that's not where they took him.

That moment is burned into my memory forever. Instead of a normal, adolescent hospital room, they wheeled my son to the oncology unit. The same unit where my friend's daughter was treated for neuroblastoma.

Instantly, I felt nauseous. That horrible mother's intuition returned. The staff tried to reassure me, explaining that they only put Nick in oncology so he could receive a higher level of care. I tried very hard to believe them, but could not.

The next two days were filled with a whirlwind of visitors and well-wishers. I had managed to slip out to get something to eat when I ran into our oncologist in the elevator. She was on her way to pick up the bone-marrow biopsy results.

I told her what the surgeons had told me—that they were optimistic that everything was benign. She gave me a funny look.

An hour later, I was standing in the hall when I saw the oncologist walking toward me. I looked at her, and I just knew. I started shaking. I said something like, "Bone marrow is positive, isn't it?"

She said, rather matter-of-factly, "Yes, it is metastatic neuroblastoma."

I collapsed on the floor.

The long, deep fall into a world that would become my new reality had begun. I had to be helped down the hall to the oncologist's office. My husband sat with me as we tried to listen to her, but my head was ringing. I pulled the trash can over and threw up, right there in her office. I was overcome with the knowledge that we absolutely had to get Nick out of that hospital. This was not going to be a carbon copy of my friend's experience. I knew we had to get to Memorial Sloan Kettering Cancer Center in New York. There, they had a specialized neuroblastoma team, with a cutting-edge neuroblastoma treatment. It was different than the treatment Nick would receive at home in Virginia. If we were going to save our son, we had to give up the life we knew, and act quickly.

In the small town we live in, word travels fast. Over the next few days, the news spread that our son had just been through an aggressive and dangerous surgery, and that we were packing up and taking him to New York City, where he would be receiving cancer treatment. The night before we left, I stayed home with Nick, while a vigil was held in our town park. Friends and family gathered near the town gazebo. The rest of my family stood in awe—the park was filled with people offering hope and love and support as bagpipes played in Nick's honor.

That same gazebo would again be filled with supporters six years later.

That night, after packing up our lives, I went into Nick's room. I asked him if he had any questions about the next day. He shook his head no. There were no words exchanged. He squeezed my hand and a tear rolled down his cheek as our eyes locked and our connection deepened.

We both knew what we had to do.

New York—August 2005

The train passed towns and water and sailboats and shopping centers. I remember seeing them go by in a blur. Nick, Jim, and I got further and further from the familiar, and closer to the city that would become our battleground. It is where Nick would stage his fight and we would learn so much as we watched him fight with humor, fortitude and grace. Just off First Avenue, Upper East Side, New York City, we checked into room 309 and officially became residents of the Ronald McDonald House. We were a team—three sets of eyes filled with fear and adjusting to our one room, with two beds. We were terrified but determined, as we pushed Nick in a wheelchair five blocks to the place that would eventually feel like a safe womb for us: Memorial Sloan Kettering Cancer Center.

There were introductions to the team, repeat testing to make sure all the initial tests were accurate, and a new test called an MIBG (meta-iodobenzylguanidine). When we met Dr. Modak, he deftly pulled up the results of the MIBG on his computer. I remember him turning the screen toward us and saying, "I'm sorry; it's positive." With absolute horror, I looked at my son's skeleton on the screen. There were bright spots sprinkled all over his body, each one indicating where the neuroblastoma had found a home in his bones. Nick was sitting there with us, so I had to keep it together. But inside, I was screaming as I felt my son—and our family—falling faster and deeper into a bottomless black hole.

We were told Nick needed to begin treatment immediately. And so, three days after arriving in a strange city with nothing familiar to anchor us, my husband and I faced reality: Our son's situation was incredibly serious. His only hope of survival was to follow the steps these doctors were telling us to follow.

Over the course of his treatment, Nick faced many awkward situations. If you've ever known a fifteen-year-old boy, you know they aren't fond of having even regular conversations. Imagine talking with a teenage boy about freezing his sperm for the future. In addition to enduring pain, fear, and a bunch of awkward, uneasy introductions to an entire team of doctors, Nick was advised to attempt to produce a sperm specimen before chemotherapy started.

I found hope in the fact that the doctors even entertained fatherhood for Nick as a future possibility.

My son Jeff had joined us in New York. Less than two weeks after his massive surgery, Nick, his brother, and his father headed to a doctor's office to take care of the sperm business. I stayed behind and couldn't help but smile as the three boys marched forward with purpose. Unfortunately, with the trauma Nick's body had been through, there would be no "activity" in his sample. They asked him to try not once, but twice, and both times another disappointment slapped us in the face. Still, he had the maturity to try.

I'm the type of person who likes to know everything there is to know about a given situation. That's a big part of my approach to life. However, that all changed when it came to *this* situation. I quickly discovered that I didn't want to know anything beyond what the doctors were telling us. I did not want to know statistics, or about other people, only about my son. I was frankly terrified.

The team of doctors told us it was crucial that Nick have an early response to treatment. Older patients with this disease often don't respond very well. Since Nick was a teenager, the doctors were not very optimistic that he would respond. Jim was brave enough to approach one of the doctors privately and ask the question I was too afraid to entertain: Was there any benefit in subjecting our son to aggressive, high-dose chemo if he was going to die anyway? The doctor explained that older patients can live for a very long time with what he called "stable" disease. To us, this was huge news. When I gently tried to explain it to Nick, he looked at both of us with indignation and said, "Did you really think I was going to die?"

I had no idea, at the time, how Nick's positive attitude would lead the way for all of us as we navigated the journey ahead.

II

The Long Road to Remission

The Compass Points of Friends and Strength

Sometimes the difference between giving up, and finding the strength to carry on, lies in the unconditional love of a friend. Like patterns etched in the sand by pounding currents, and the ebb and flow of the tide, a walk of strength requires constant change. A friend can be that strength through the constant change that crisis brings. Side by side a friend will stand with you, when the currents feel too strong to bear on your own. You learn to be brave and find the strength to keep breathing as friends literally breathe for you, while you find your own breath again.

When Nick started treatment, none of us really understood the intensity of what lay ahead. Most cancer protocols call for a single day of chemo every three weeks. The protocol that seemed so promising for Nick would force him to endure five straight days of high-dose therapy every three weeks, along with a long list of challenging chemo side effects. This became our life for nine months.

The reality, the rawness, the desperation settled inside me. It had been weeks since I had been able to eat more than a nibble and take a sip of tea.

Eggs Benedict and Laundry

Before Nick finished his first round of chemo, the side effects started to kick in. Low blood counts, lack of appetite, constant nausea, and weight loss became the new normal. Despite his suffering, I saw this as a good sign. His body was responding to the hideous poison. That was our first hurdle. Although he was completely wiped out, Nick still managed to maintain his loving, sweet attitude. He began to stake out a little bit of independence, declaring that he would be doing his own "dressing changes" on his chest lines and would be giving himself the shots the doctors prescribed to boost his white blood cells. I desperately wanted to hover over him and dote on him and treat him like a little boy—because he *was* my little boy. I let the tears fall in private, watching him bravely embrace his new routine of sterile fields and syringes.

One day my phone rang—a friend from home was visiting the city. She invited me out to breakfast. Jim stayed with Nick and I got a morning out. I can still remember the taste of the food. I ate a full serving of eggs benedict and experienced the satisfaction of feeling full for the first time in weeks. I cried tears of gratitude and thanked my friend for helping me cross over for a few moments into the normal world. She allowed me the luxury of food and a conversation outside of the nightmare I was living.

After breakfast, my friend came back to our room. I napped while she did all our laundry. It was such a treat—I felt like I had been to a day spa. I was just beginning to learn one small part of what would become my reality: *Caregivers must come up for air.* Nick wanted that for me too. He was constantly telling me that I was too skinny. When I told him he was too, he just looked at me and said, "Yeah, well, I have chemo. What's your excuse?"

Pancakes, Insurance, and Tacos

Nick finished his first round of chemo and we settled in back at the Ronald McDonald House. We tried to create our new family routine, consisting of meals, rest, and passing time. Through those weeks, our family—those people connected to us by blood or by friendship—helped us all navigate through the trauma.

One morning, when our schedule was blissfully free from appointments, we pulled the thick, room-darkening motel curtains shut, and slept until ten thirty in the morning! It was hard to remember the last time that happened. I felt so good, and I got inspired to make Nick pancakes. I went down to the community kitchenette and opened up my lone, small cabinet to retrieve the box of pancake mix. It turned out that a lot of the other mothers had the same idea. I had to jockey for position on the counter and then realized I didn't have a bowl to mix the batter.

I looked around the room at the other mothers. Everyone was focused on their own breakfast creations. No one seemed interested in talking, much less in sharing their bowls. I found a cooking pot and used it as a makeshift bowl. Since I didn't have any oil or shortening, I used my one stick of butter to grease the pan.

Okay, so it wasn't Saturday morning at home—but it was us having pancakes together! Despite the continual nausea that was his new normal, Nick still managed to keep a couple of pancakes down and drink a little bit of a vanilla smoothie. I mentally calculated how many calories he consumed and prayed they stayed in.

That afternoon, Nick relaxed in the sun in front of our window and did two puzzles from a crossword puzzle book. Jim and I went on a mission to find some kitchen supplies to hoard away in our room—and to fill Nick's prescription for an anti-nausea drug that would help him keep any future pancakes down!

Unfortunately, that tiny bit of peace of mind came at a high price. Our insurance only covered twenty percent of the cost of the drug. Those twenty anti-nausea tablets cost us $684.00. The experience plunged me into depression. For the next hour, I worried not only about Nick's health, but about what this whole ordeal was going to do to our family financially.

Thank God for my husband. Jim reminded me that we needed to live for what was important at that moment, and not to worry about what we couldn't do anything about. As we learned to do countless times when feeling punched in the gut, we reset our compass, picked up tacos (Nick's request), and sat up on the rooftop terrace eating and laughing. Nick managed to finish a whole chicken taco minus hot sauce and some chips that he said actually settled his tummy. Jim bought me a beer, a no-no at the "house." Nick was amused to see us breaking the rules. He said if I drank my beer fast, he would drink all of the hydration drink I was constantly nagging him to finish. I happily did my duty, and he slowly sipped with a smile on his face. Jim and I exchanged glances, and for one magical moment, we felt like a normal family sharing a special evening together- like nothing was wrong in our world.

Wheelchairs and Buddies from Home—Labor Day Weekend, 2005

Living in New York with a cancer patient taught me something I didn't know about myself: I suck at pushing a wheelchair. We were at the day clinic to check Nick's white blood cell count. That count had dropped to zero, which is very dangerous. Jim had gone to pick up two of Nick's best friends (who were visiting for the first time) at the train station. Nick and I were left on our own. Adjusting to the fact that this was our first day with no white blood cells, I looked around the clinic to discover that our wheelchair was gone.

There was no way Nick could walk the five blocks back to the "house" in his weakened condition. I managed to find a wheelchair in a closet, but since Jim was usually our wheelchair navigator, I didn't exactly know how to maneuver it. To make matters worse, when we got out on the street, we discovered that one of the leg rests was broken. Every time we hit a patch of road or sidewalk that wasn't perfectly level (which happens every time you enter an intersection), the chair scraped the ground and pitched Nick forward, almost hurling him to the ground.

Picture, if you will, this scene on First Avenue, New York City. Nick's head buried in his hands as I get down on my hands and knees in the intersection, pretending I know how to fix the stupid thing. It turns out I didn't. Even though he was tired and irritated, Nick managed to be patient with me. Finally, despite his exhaustion, he opted to get out and walk at every intersection rather than be thrown repeatedly into the street by his well-meaning mom. To add insult to injury, he also had to wear a mask in public to guard against germs attacking his completely vulnerable immune system. That did *not* make him happy.

And that was just the start of our day.

The day got a little brighter, and although he was exhausted, he greeted his friends with high fives and hugs. Soon, the boys were chillin' just like they did at home. Jim and I found a first-floor lounge with a huge fish tank. I zonked out on a couch while Jim did the *New York Times* crossword puzzle.

That night, Nick felt very tired and queasy, so his friends watched TV while he slept. Years later, I still marvel at the courage and love it took for those two teenage boys to walk into Nick's world and instinctively know how to just "be" with him. *Sometimes, just being a strong and silent presence makes all the difference.*

Five of us were cramped in room 309 that night and it was tight. Jim and I took a walk up Third Avenue and blended in to the scene, window shopping and just wandering for a bit. We looked just like everyone else on the street. The irony struck me—as people passed by enjoying their holiday weekend plans, we were busy learning how *not* to plan beyond our next few hours.

On Sunday morning, the boys were anxious to see a little of the real New York, beyond the five-block neighborhood between the Ronald McDonald House and the hospital. Since Nick was still too weak to walk, they decided to wheel him around the city and look for a golf store. I was shocked when Nick agreed to it, once again accepting his circumstances and making the best of them. I remember watching them cross First Avenue, pushing Nick, chatting away as if nothing was wrong. That was the first time I had seen Nick enjoy the slightest bit of freedom away from Jim or me in over a month. My heart filled with gratitude at the sight.

All weekend long Jim and I kept looking at each other, silently aching, but smiling at the same time. *We were so proud of Nick's friends for taking their last weekend before school started to travel to New York just to be with him. We witnessed beautiful, real, and honest life moments...connecting heart to heart, friend to friend. If you think about it, that's what life is all about—human connection.*

Fever and Five Block Cab Rides

Jim went back to Virginia to get some work done. I was doing caretaker duty alone, and so far, it was going fine. I was tucked into bed, my hands tapping away on the computer keys, connecting to my "other world."

Then I heard those dreaded words, "Oops, I have a temperature."

A neutropenic fever can cause an infection that ravages the body swiftly. Life and death can be quickly decided by how quickly IV antibiotics are started. Nick's fever was 100.5, and he suddenly started having chills. I could tell he was scared. I was terrified.

I had to dress and pack quickly for the hospital. I walked with Nick to the corner and hailed a cab, ten at night in a strange city. His teeth were chattering as he leaned on me, wrapped in a blanket that did nothing to stop the shivering. A cabbie quickly pulled over, but he was not happy to learn that we were only going five blocks. However, after seeing the panic in my eyes, and Nick's shaking body, he changed his mind. He let us in and took off, fast, arriving at the emergency room entrance in less than two minutes.

Later, coping with these fevers would become routine. But that night, it was another new experience that had us both wide-eyed and terrified of the unknown. I felt exhausted, frustrated, and, with Jim gone, a bit lonely. I had to get a grip and regroup. That meant getting into the next routine of setting up camp in the hospital. The constant change was unnerving, but it was the new way we had to live. Later, as Nick drifted off to sleep in his hospital bed, he reached out and held my hand. I felt the blessed energy of mother and son, connected in a surreal way, doing the best we could.

Angel Barbara

Having a sick child introduced me to many new things, including the incredible kindness of strangers. People we had never met before often reached out to us and offered help, sometimes becoming the most intimate of friends in the process. Angel Barbara was one of those people.

Barbara lives half a block from the Ronald McDonald House. She has dedicated her life to being a sort of "family away from home" for the kids and families who come to New York for treatment. Over the years, she has developed a huge network of restaurants, salons, stores, and more around the city, all willing to do kind and generous things for the families she meets.

My friend who had lived in New York when her daughter was undergoing neuroblastoma treatment let Barbara know we were there. When she showed up, in true, New York-minute style, it was like a dream came true. She arranged a day at a salon for me to have my hair done and then walked to Bed, Bath and Beyond to buy Nick a special pillow and egg crate mattress pad so his body didn't sweat from the plastic and vinyl coverings on his bed—a trick she picked up just by helping other families.

In a city of strangers, it was wonderful to find a new friend. *As I learned repeatedly throughout Nick's illness, the world is full of angels.*

Caryn Franca

Massages and Backpacks

Monday at Sloan Kettering was usually the day for new patients to arrive. It seemed like every week I would witness another red-eyed mother experiencing the same raw, unexplainable grief that ripped me when I first realized our lives had changed forever. One woman walked in with her son—a tall, handsome young man who looked totally healthy. By the end of the day, he left, hooked up to his backpack of chemicals just like ours. His mom looked vacant, distraught, and scared.

It was the same routine every week. We walked in Monday morning feeling strong, but by seven in the evening, when we all left for the day, we would walk out totally drained. We pushed our precious children in strollers and wheelchairs, with backpacks filled with IV fluids and hydration bags. We waited at the elevators, eyes mostly staring straight ahead. Each mother or father was struggling to stay strong and push forward, hoping that their child would be one of the ones that made it through this hell.

One particular Monday, Nick returned to our room at the "House" completely exhausted. He wasn't throwing up, but felt really sick. Jim offered to massage his feet, and Nick shut his eyes and said he was imagining he was on a beach in Hawaii. For a few minutes, he forgot about the chemo and where he was. He reached out to hold our hands, and we started massaging his hands. Nick said it was one of the best feelings he had ever had.

At times like those, when Nick was at his weakest, he would tell us he loved us a lot. That night, he also admitted that he was trying to be funny and make us smile so that we wouldn't be so worried about him. That was his way. We all slept feeling very close and connected that night.

When morning came, we grabbed the blue canvas backpack with the tubes that provided hydration and medicine and headed back to the clinic. We hung the backpack from a pole on the wheelchair and left with enough time to reach the clinic by eight o'clock. We walked the five blocks back to the hospital at the same time the neighborhood kids were leaving for their normal days at school—with their normal, school backpacks. The contrast between Nick's chemo backpack and those school backpacks was vivid. Some of the children would stare. Nick hung his head and covered himself with his blanket. Slumped over with a throw-up pan in his hand, Jim and I kept our eyes straight ahead. It seemed we were always trying to be brave and not cry. As we watched all the beautiful, happy children walking to school, we blinked back tears, wondering if our son would ever get to do that again.

A Weekend of Joy, Sadness, and Fun

Joy

One Saturday morning I was awakened by the phone. The lobby had a flower delivery for me to sign for. Since Jim looks much better in the morning than I do, I convinced him to stumble out of bed and go get the flowers. He came back five minutes later with my daughter, son-in-law, and granddaughter! They had driven up the night before, stayed with a friend from high school, and found their way to us on Saturday morning. It was an amazing, wonderful surprise.

Friends from college were going out of town that weekend and offered us their house. After hanging out all morning, we all piled into the minivan and found our way to Bronxville. Nick was so grateful to see trees and a yard, and a couch, and a real kitchen—and space to be alone. He relaxed, we got carry-out for dinner and settled in to watch a movie.

At moments like that, we could almost forget. It was a taste of normalcy blanketed with joy, surreal but welcome.

Sadness

At four in the morning my daughter woke me up. Nick was calling for me. I found him retching violently on the bathroom floor. The nausea was a deep, awful, exhausting full-body experience that left him weak and frail. For the first time, he said he didn't know if he could endure nine months of this horror. I told him I would take it from him if I could. He said it would kill him to see me like him. Then, somehow, Nick found this amazing strength. He said, "Mom, this is just what is meant to be for me right now." I couldn't hold back the tears. I snuggled next to him on the bathroom floor and patted his back, and eventually, he was able to drift back to sleep.

On Sunday morning, he woke up very tired, but still had the energy to take a walk. He marveled at the homes, the trees, the quiet contrast from our city dwellings. Peeking in the windows of the houses we walked past, I wondered if there were people inside alone and suffering. I wondered what their stories were, and as I walked next to my weak-yet-determined son, I wondered what they saw looking out at us. If only they knew our story of love, of strength, of a family united, hoping and praying for a miracle.

Fun

We had tickets to see the New York Rangers play ice hockey back in the city that night. Unfortunately, Nick got another bout of nausea just before we were set to leave. Jim said he would stay back with him until he felt better. At the end of the first period I looked up and there he was. My brave, bald boy was heading to his seat, with puke bucket in hand and fierce resolve in his eyes. As he sat down my heart broke at the scene that had become our life. Despite it all, Nick cheered and smiled and was happy to have had a weekend so full of love and family and support.

That was what kept us all going.

Perspective and Gratitude

As difficult and painful as my life had become, there were times when I still felt spoiled—especially when I met people who were experiencing what I was experiencing alone, with no support network. I met a single dad who was raising his fifteen-year-old son who had a tumor in his leg, and a thirteen-year-old daughter, coping all on his own. He lived two hours away. He would go home and make casseroles, clean the house, and make arrangements for his daughter. Then he would head back to the Ronald McDonald House to deal with his son, and chemo and wheelchairs. He did it all, he did it by himself, and somehow he always had a positive attitude.

Then there were women from other countries who didn't speak the language. Some had three or four kids sharing a room with them (sometimes for years) with no neighbors, friends, or family to hold their hands. My life felt like a nightmare, but there were times when I felt so lucky. I saw so many people with less support than I had.

I decided to try and maintain my sanity and my sense of faith by listing at least five things each day that I was grateful for. This was my list on the first day:

1. Nick having a day of rest and no nausea.
2. A cup of coffee, and a walk in the beautiful weather, with a friend of twenty-nine years and another friend of four weeks.
3. A cousin, who is like a sister to me, who overcame her fear of needles to donate platelets for Nick.
4. Having two parents who are still alive and care enough to come next week, even though the city is big and unfamiliar to them.
5. Two sons, a son-in-law, a daughter, a granddaughter, and a husband who all breathe every breath with the same love and faith and support that I do.
6. Nick going down to the kitchen of the "House" to bring *me* ice cream in bed while we played cards.
7. Friends who show up, even when they don't know what to say or how to act around bald children.
8. Doctors and nurses who are becoming like family to us.

We were learning a new rhythm to live by, one that gave us some sense of cadence and pattern. Chaos and terror were replaced by gratitude, purpose, and the new normal of living through rounds of chemotherapy.

Visiting the Place We Call Home

Between Nick's rounds of treatment, there were brief periods when we were able to jump on the train and head south for a few days back home. The first trip back was the hardest-welcome but painful.

We passed by Nick's high school, then the stop sign, then took two more turns, and then....we were home. Pulling up, things appeared the same—lamps in the windows, dogs on the porch. A false, surreal sense of normal tricked me for a minute.

With suitcases, backpacks, and plastic bags full of meds, we opened the door to our previous life. Immediately, I felt lost, undone, and fragile. Home was supposed to be my sanctuary, but I felt none of that. Instead, my daily routine of survival felt intruded upon and interrupted by this glimpse of what I left behind. My comfort was now in New York, woven into a blanket of blood checks, clinic visits, and walking to the corner for coffee. Somehow, there was a sense of security in those simple routines. It gave me a bar to measure progress, and progress was all that mattered.

I was surprised to find that I needed to learn to see home as the *real* life we were striving so hard to get back to. It was the ultimate goal and the prize, not just for Nick, but for all of us. Those brief respites of home needed to become part of the healing process, not just a trip back to an open wound where the last days of our other life resided.

That first night back, my daughter prepared a candlelight dinner with white roses and white tablecloths on our back porch. We were all glad to reconnect around a prayer and a family meal. And it helped. My sense of self grew a little stronger. I felt powerful love enveloping our family as we blessed the food together. That night we all slept in our own beds, and finally, the weekend we had highly anticipated began to unfold with love and joy.

The time went quickly, with friends and family surrounding us. There were experiences for Nick that strengthened his soul. During an evening at our cousin's house, he asked to spend the night there. I had to really fight internally, to not go into an overprotective mode. I had to get outside of my needs and focus on Nick's—a very hard dance for a worried and emotionally exhausted mother to do. I overcame my fear and said, "Cool, see you in the morning. Love you." It was the first time I had been physically separated from my child overnight in two months. That terrified me.

When the visit was over and we were headed back to New York on the train, I reflected on our three days of "normal." The time at home had been such a gift. I was grateful for those days, for the time, for all the people who continued to hold us up, enabling us to continue to do the best that we could do as we walked this path. Time at home gave us a much needed perspective. It gave Nick a sense of confidence that he could still live and feel like himself without a lot of barriers. Cancer was the name of something very wrong in Nick's body. But, cancer didn't take away the spirit of life that was so strong in this beautiful young man. I will forever call my son my hero.

That weekend at home made me realize that life is nothing more than moments linked together to make hours, days, months, and years. We don't know how many of those moments each of us gets. We decide what to make of them—it is entirely our choice. Nick made it clear that he was choosing to not drown in self-pity, but to seize every moment he felt good and make the most of them.

I hope we can all learn to live more like that.

The Mad-o-Meter

Despite everything he was going through, Nick didn't really see himself as "sick." He viewed the invasion of his body as an inconvenience to be dealt with. His spirits were up—so ours needed to be as well. We were learning that the mind has an amazing way of prompting the body to respond when negative thoughts are not accepted. We wanted to follow Nick's lead to banish all negative energy from our world.

Nick returned from our weekend at home with renewed energy for a new round of chemo. This round involved drugs that would cause even more nausea. While he was waiting to get started, a sweet, young child-life specialist popped her head around the curtain. She suggested Nick visit the "teen room," as they were going to do a project. Nick politely declined, and when she left, he rolled his eyes.

He then announced that he would do a project on his own.

He grabbed his empty water bottle, a latex glove, and some medical tape. He blew into the glove so the fingers filled with air, and then taped the latex "hand" to the water bottle. He then took a sharpie and wrote on the water bottle:

"Nick's Mad-o-Meter"
All fingers up, I am happy.
Middle finger up, leave me alone.

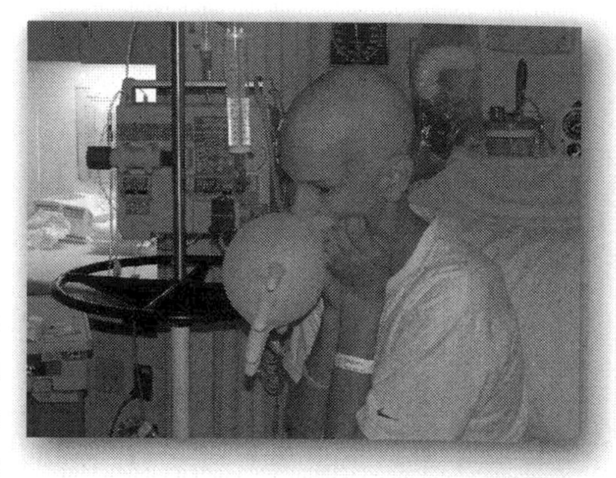

Nick's sense of humor remained one of the things we were most grateful for. I knew that half the time he was making jokes to protect the people who loved him from worry—and the thing was, it *worked*. We found immense joy in each and every moment when Nick was able to find humor in the hell he was living through. That was especially true as the awful side effects from the new round of chemo took hold. The week of treatment was even more brutal than we anticipated. Nick spent most of his time sleeping or being pushed up and down First Avenue in his wheelchair, head hanging low into his puke pan.

Watching our child suffer, our thoughts would wander to dark places where they shouldn't go. Our questions were more magnified, and our fears more vivid. What was happening to our son? Would it ever end? While he slept one evening after treatment, Jim and I slipped around the corner to a little Indian restaurant for a talk I still remember today. The subject was our constant challenge with faith.

Nick's illness was testing our faith to an almost unimaginable degree. We were so angry. We wondered aloud, "Why do miracles need to happen at all? Why didn't God simply intervene before the horror of cancer took over and made a miracle necessary? Why did God create healing instead of intervening before illness took place?" We held hands across the table, quietly acknowledging our bottomless ache for answers, the answers we could not find.

Faith is trusting, even when there are no answers the human brain can provide.

Unconditional Love, Wrapped in Humor

Despite the challenges his father and I were experiencing, Nick was always Nick. One night during this especially challenging period, Jim—who rarely wrote—was moved to the point where he wrote the following:

> *Home from the last day of this horrific round of chemo, Nick just fell into his bed. I turned on the TV music station to a meditative background. He enjoyed the music and there was a sense of tranquility in room 309.*
>
> *Caryn lay down in the bed next to his (only 10 inches or so away) and was holding his hand. Not wanting to be left out of the action, I laid down next to Caryn and all was quiet and peaceful. We were there for about 10 minutes and I thought both Nick and Caryn were napping.*
>
> *I thought I could get away with passing a teeny little gas thing.*
>
> *After a few seconds, out of a seeming dead sleep Nick piped up, "There goes the mood." Caryn and I laughed out loud, not only at his perfect sense of dry humor timing, but also out of relief—relief that he is who he is in this awful mess.*
>
> *A little while later, Nick started to hiccup. The hiccups are a slight annoyance for most of us, but when you are getting chemo, hiccups often become more violent than is comfortable. In addition to lasting interminably long, they bring on nausea. So, after a little personal time with his yellow bucket, Nick laid back down and asked Caryn and I to snuggle in his bed with him.*
>
> *I cannot describe the beauty, the closeness, the unconditional LOVE, that we experienced. Nick's words after we had been lying peacefully and quietly together for quite some time said it all. "THIS IS ALL THE MEDICINE I NEED."*

The gift of that hour is something I will cherish. I can't imagine another circumstance that would prompt mother, son and father to ball up like bear cubs and lay in total peace and contentment. I don't understand where Nick gets his enormous strength and spirit; his ability to find peace and contentment in this situation, but we are blessed and grateful for it.

A Phone Call and a Hug

Despite Nick's amazing fortitude, the chemo treatments grew more and more difficult, pushing my strong, determined son to the point where he was almost ready to give up. Naturally, watching my child get pushed to the edge pushed me to the edge. I tried to be strong, but sometimes I couldn't keep from breaking down. Although I knew in my heart that there was no answer, I still couldn't help screaming inside; *Why my son? Why?*

I poured those feelings out in an especially desperate phone call to my cousin. Her son, Greg, and Nick were like brothers—just ten months apart and very close. After she and I got off the phone, she drove straight to the high school, pulled her son out of class, and put him on the next train to New York City, telling him that Nick needed him for strength. Six hours later, Greg walked into the hospital room where Nick was sleeping and tapped him on the shoulder. Nick opened his eyes and, realizing who it was, opened his arms wide. Tears rolled down my cheeks for what had to be the tenth time that day as the two of them embraced. Later, armed with every anti-nausea medication known to man, along with three backpacks full of fluids, Greg pushed Nick's wheelchair out of hell, and together, we walked into a weekend of love.

I will forever be grateful to Nick's friends (who grew up in suburban comfort in Virginia) for learning to navigate the northbound train from Washington DC and to hail New York cabs on their own. They were always there for Nick—they always showed up, they always knew just how to be. I know they are better, wiser men today because of how they chose not to walk away, but to embrace Nick's journey by his side.

Scans, Tests, and Nerves

After a certain number of chemo rounds have been completed, the doctors perform surgery to remove the tumor that chemo has killed. They do a set of scans and bone-marrow biopsies before the operation to see how the body has responded in eradicating the cancer.

Waiting for results was always especially excruciating, so I concentrated (or tried to concentrate) on the following:

- Learning to be flexible
- Learning to be patient
- Learning to control fear
- Learning gratitude for small joys

The small joy of the moment was Nick lying in the bed next to me, allowing me to rub his back, as we imagined the pre-surgery test results being only good news.

Then we received a small miracle. Two of our nurse practitioners called—on the phone together—to share the excitement that there was a significant change in Nick's bone marrow! The preliminary biopsy results looked good, and we would be able to move forward with surgery on Monday.

I hung up the phone and literally wandered the halls of the Ronald McDonald House with tears rolling down my face. I found myself on the first floor, in the chapel, on my knees thanking God for being the instrument to create miracles.

Nick and Jim were not as enthusiastic. I asked Nick if he was excited, and he said in his very laid-back way, "When it's over I'll be happy."

We were able to head home for a few days to rest and prepare for the nine hour operation. After our weekend at home, sitting on the train heading back to New York, images of the weekend flashed through my mind:

- My precious granddaughter with her open arms, squealing my name when she saw me.
- Nick with his beautiful smile laughing with his friends.

- A sea of faces at a golf tournament held in Nick's honor. Some people we'd known for years and some we just met, all there to support us.
- Coffee and girl talk at Starbucks with one of my dearest friends.
- Touching my golf clubs for the first time since I was pulled off the course in August with the awful news that Nick's scans looked like cancer.
- Playing nine holes of golf after a dear friend encouraged me to do something for myself. Then, after a few emotional moments of transition, actually laughing and relaxing for a couple of hours.
- Family dinners together.
- Hugs from my parents.
- Falling asleep *before* Nick got in from the Friday night football game, knowing he was out having a blast with his friends.

Surgery was successful. The amazing Dr. Michael Laquaglia removed the tumor from Nick's psoas muscle. He also removed a piece that was five inches long and an inch thick that was wrapped near his aortic artery. He was really pleased with how much he was able to remove. What was left did not light up on the scan he performed after the surgery. Removing that small piece would have surely paralyzed him and we were relieved it didn't light up on the scan.

Successful yes, but the surgery was also major. The incision went around Nick's side and partially across his abdomen, so they could reach the bulk of the tumor. After the operation, he was a little swollen and in severe pain. They usually do an epidural block for that type of surgery, but the spot where they typically give the block was exactly where they had to operate. Still, even though he was hurting and strongly medicated, when we first saw Nick in recovery, he flashed the peace sign to Jim and held his fist out to do a fist bump. The surgeon assisting Dr. Laquaglia remarked that he had never seen a stronger human being.

I was numb, but had a peaceful, thankful feeling inside—thankful for our amazing surgeons, thankful for our amazingly strong son, and thankful for all of the friends and family that literally helped us breathe every step of the way. Another scan was done post-surgery to see if the bony lesions were less bright, or hope against hope—not visible!

Thanksgiving 2005

We anxiously awaited the post-surgery scan results while preparing to spend our first-ever Thanksgiving in New York. Nick had recovered well. Ten days later it was the night before Thanksgiving. We boarded a bus with the rest of the Ronald McDonald House residents. We were privileged to go see the famous Macy's Thanksgiving Day Parade balloon floats.

While sitting on the bus, my cell phone rang. It was the hospital number. An electric surge of fear jolted through my body—doctors don't usually call unless it's bad news. With Jim and Nick sitting blissfully unaware a couple of seats ahead of me, I answered the phone. Our primary team doctor, Dr. Kushner, was on the other end. He was actually giggly. He wanted us all to know that Nick's scan was negative for disease. He wanted us to have the news before Thanksgiving so we could enjoy it.

I was shaking as I shared the news with Jim and Nick. I could have shouted it out to the whole bus—a bus filled with families and children all battling cancer far away from home. I knew that even though we were strangers, everyone would have cheered for us. Everyone had experienced the terror of scan results. We all knew that sometimes, those results did not produce joy.

So, I kept the news to just us.

When we got back to the "House," my children and granddaughter had arrived from Virginia. I felt such a sense of completeness and peace, more than I had felt since our ordeal began in August. We all slept in one room, room 309, all seven of us packed in sleeping bags and rollaway beds.

The next day we were treated to an amazing blessing. A dear friend from home had arranged for my family to spend Thanksgiving at her cousin's apartment a few blocks from the Ronald McDonald House. Her cousin was out of town for Thanksgiving and had offered her home to us—perfect strangers—so that our family could enjoy the holiday in a homey environment.

When we arrived, she had already set a stunning table with her finest china and silver. Two bottles of wine were chilled and waiting, and loving notes urging us to make ourselves completely at home were posted.

I cried as I took it all in.

Once again, the spirit and generosity from friends and strangers helped our family walk down the difficult road we were traveling with a little more strength and fortitude. As we gathered around the table, we held hands and gave thanks to God for his everlasting presence, embodied and channeled through these strangers, who were now friends we hadn't even met.

Even as we sometimes reject and question His hand on us, it is always there.

We stayed in the apartment for the entire weekend, celebrating Nick's sixteenth birthday a little early because all of our family and some dear friends were there. Nick made a wish and blew out his candles, and we all were thankful. I spent that weekend thinking about everything we had to be thankful for. *In the midst of the war we were fighting, there were so many unexpected blessings.*

A Bath, a Prayer, and Confetti from God

After a beautiful Thanksgiving, we returned to reality—another round of aggressive chemotherapy. The weather grew colder, and the days shorter and darker. It was the beginning of a dark and lonely period. Nick was really struggling, trying to eat and fight the nausea in hopes that he could gain enough weight to avoid supplemental IV nutrition. But as hard as he worked, there was so little he could control. He was angry and frustrated and his spirits dropped. I struggled so hard to say the "right" things and hoped Nick heard them the "right" way. But sometimes, there is no "right" thing to say. So, I rubbed Nick's back and prayed out loud as he tried to relax and get his mind together. He told me that it felt good. Then, after a bath, we prayed together again before Nick drifted off to sleep. I sat there in the dark, watching him, my baby. A tear ran down my face. Maybe we were finally turning the corner. Maybe he was going to get better.

I stepped out of the room for a few minutes When I returned, Jim was kneeling by Nick, holding his hands and praying. I think they both were crying. I wasn't quite sure what to do, so I just curled up on Nick's other side and starting praying too. I found out later Nick had been having a horrible hiccup attack that made him even more nauseous and hurt his incision from surgery. They had been praying for the hiccups to end and for Nick to be peaceful and calm. And it worked. They told me they had shared a little miracle together. I was so moved.

We spent Nick's sixteenth birthday in room 309 in the Ronald McDonald House, playing a game, trying to eat, and feeling love and gratitude for another year. Looking out onto Seventy-Third Street, it looked like winter. Nick told me he hoped for snow on his birthday—we would pretend God was throwing confetti down for us to celebrate the beauty of Nick's life.

Hailing Cabs in the Night

By this time, Nick had taken total and complete charge of his medical routines—hooking up his own IV bags, flushing his lines, changing his caps and dressings, and injecting himself with white cell stimulator. I was in awe, "overseeing" it all as he took care of everything. I wondered what my now sixteen-year-old son was learning about himself, and about life, this year in which he was receiving no formal education. I prayed that he would grow to be a young man who would know how to love unconditionally, have compassion, accept people, and never ever stop believing in miracles. Those are just some of the skills that develop naturally living in a house filled with kids who look odd, suffer greatly, and fight hard.

By now we knew that eleven days after the start of a round of chemo, we could expect Nick to get a fever. Just like clockwork, at one in the morning, he woke up saying he was cold and had chills. Jim was back in Virginia at work, and I had just finally gotten into a good sleep after a rough day. I took Nick's temperature, and since it was still normal, we agreed to ride it out and see if we could wait until morning.

That lasted two hours, by which point his temperature had climbed to 101.7.

So...what's a mother stuck at a Ronald McDonald House, in the middle of the night, in the middle of New York City, to do?

Luckily, I had packed a suitcase before going to bed, just in case. Nick was shaking so hard from the fever that he was unable to walk. I helped him into a wheelchair, wheeled him out the door and pushed him fifty yards to the corner of First Avenue and hailed a cab. Except...the wheelchair we used wouldn't fold up to fit into the cab. I sat Nick down on top of the suitcase, wrapped him in a blanket, ran the wheelchair back to Ronald McDonald House, and then ran back. By this time my son looked like a little old homeless man crouched under his blanket. We caught a cab to the hospital and arrived in the emergency room completely exhausted. Nick looked up at me, flashed me a thumbs-up and said, "We got here!"

It was classic Nick to act like the previous two hours had been no big deal.

Friends, Nosebleeds, and Compassion

With Christmas approaching, three long-time friends came up from Virginia to donate platelets for Nick, do my laundry at the Ronald McDonald House, and decorate our door for the holiday. They took me out for a lovely dinner, but when I got back to Nick's hospital room, he was feeling off. Soon afterward, he got a nosebleed that would become legendary as the worst anyone on the ninth floor at Sloan Kettering could remember.

Chemo can deplete the body of platelets, and without adequate platelets to clot your blood, nosebleeds can become serious very quickly. They aren't a common side effect of chemo, but then again nothing about Nick, nor his side effects, were common! In fact, stopping Nick's nosebleed required five people hovering around him, a rapid infusion of platelets to help his blood clot, and an ENT (ear, nose, and throat specialist) to pack his nose. It took most of the night, during which he lost a lot of blood, and we got very little sleep.

The next morning, my girlfriends came by the hospital with coffee and a muffin for me. Since Nick was so exhausted, I didn't want them to come into the room, so I met them outside. When I came back, Nick called me over and pulled me close. He whispered to me that he felt bad about how loud we had been the night before.

He was worried about his roommate—a twelve-year-old boy who was in a bed on the other side of the curtain. Nick noticed that no one had stayed overnight with the boy, and he didn't seem to have a mother. He asked, "Why don't you go over and ask him if he would like some hot chocolate or something?"

With a packed nose and multiple infusions of blood and platelets, after a sleepless night, Nick was thinking about his roommate.

My precious son, I love him so.

"Survivor" and Reflections

On the ninth floor of Sloan Kettering, in our now-familiar home on the inpatient ward, Nick and I watched the *Survivor* finale. One of the finalists said, "Playing the game of *Survivor* is the hardest game you could ever play, physically, mentally, and emotionally." Calmly but powerfully, Nick shared his own thoughts on the subject. He said, "No, the game of life is the hardest game you'll ever play."

The world on the inpatient floor felt so closed in. Parents, like Jim and me, walked the halls, pushing strollers or wheelchairs with IV poles. There were strangers reaching out to each other, eager residents doing their rounds, and kind nurses who always seemed to be smiling and filled with optimism. There was hope, and there was despair. This had become my world. It was like a weird type of jail—an institution where everyone had lost something precious and valuable—their sense of control over their own lives.

I wondered, *How would I come out on the other side? Who would I be? What would really be important to me?*

Illness brings a wisdom all its own—a wisdom that teaches patience, tolerance, and a new sense of value for the moments that make up life. Historians and pundits often talk about how, as Americans, we collectively lost our innocence on 9/11. Cancer was like that for my family. It took our innocence. It reminded us that no one is ever truly safe. The unthinkable can happen to anyone at any time.

I looked back at pictures of Nick from just a few months before, from the spring and summer before he got sick, and I felt like I knew a totally different person. I wasn't sure if it was because Nick had changed so much, or because, as horrible as the past months had been, they had also given me an opportunity to get to know my youngest child in an entirely different way. Cancer bonded us at a level few parents ever experience with their children. That was one of the unexpected gifts of Nick's illness; I felt like I knew his soul—and that was a great privilege.

A Letter of Love from My Husband

As the year drew to a close, our friends and relatives engaged in the annual tradition of composing their lighthearted, news-filled Christmas letters. Our family's letter, which Jim wrote, was a little different:

Dear Friends,

I did not want this year to end without acknowledging all you have done for us these past months. We have been facing the greatest challenge of our lives, so far, and all of you have been there with us the whole way. You will never know how much it has meant to us to have you with us. You are part of us in a most real way.

I also did not want to let any more time go by without saying something about Caryn.

I will never forget the day we learned of Nick's cancer. The image of Caryn sobbing on the floor of the oncologist's office and shaking uncontrollably is burned into my memory. The news was obviously devastating, but, all the more so, because our surgeons had told us that Nick's tumor was benign. We were so relieved, then came the word of the bone marrow infection, stage IV neuroblastoma.

Caryn allowed herself about 30 minutes of pity, then she did what we have all come to know is her trademark, she took action. Arrangements were made for Nick to be treated at Memorial Sloan Kettering Cancer Center in NYC, a decision she was absolutely sure about, one that probably saved his life. She knew what needed to be done, and she made sure it was. SOOOOO Caryn!!!!!!

Throughout this ordeal, she has been the rock. She knows exactly when and how to push Nick, and when to let him take the lead. He has responded by becoming a man way before his time. Thanks to Caryn's lead, he changes his own dressings, flushes his chemo port himself, knows all of his medications, and advocates for himself with the nurses, doctors and his parents.

One of the most difficult things for me, as a parent, has been the speeding up of the maturation process for Nick. He should be worrying about pimples and his driver's license, not chemo ports and nausea medications. Mom has made it as easy for him as possible, teaching when necessary, urging, and when appropriate, demanding. She always puts his needs first, paying little or no attention to hers, even if it makes him mad at her.

This has been a dark cloud we are under, very dark. But like all clouds it does have a silver lining, that is you. Though the cloud is very dark, it is not as dark as you are bright.

As we get ready to come back home for Xmas, we are thankful that you have supported us. The unbearable has been tolerated, we have been cushioned by your aid, and we have done the best we could for Nick. These things were accomplished, in part, thanks to you, all of you, and especially because of CARYN.

I wish you the happiest of holidays, and the return of the LOVE you have given,

Jim

Home for Christmas and the Promise of a Happy New Year

After four months of calling the third floor of the Ronald McDonald House home, we returned to our own home for Christmas. Nick slept for most of the trip. I thought about what we were leaving behind, and how different the pulse of Christmas felt.

When we pulled up into our gravel driveway, we were greeted by a beautiful scene. Jim had done all the decorating the week before and managed to keep it a secret from me. The house was lit with colored lights, and through the dining room window, I could see candles burning, a red tablecloth on the dining table, and twinkle lights everywhere! Walking inside, I saw that every decoration I had collected over twenty-five years was displayed somewhere. The tree was decorated, the stockings were hung, and the house was full. It was beautiful.

Saying goodnight to Nick that night, he looked at me and simply said, "Doesn't it feel good to be here?"

New Year's Day, 2006

As I looked ahead to 2006, I saw a year that held so much hope for us. I knew I had a choice. I could ring in the New Year with fear of the unknown in my heart. Or, I could face 2006 with steadfast hope and optimism. I could wallow in sadness over having to return to New York City and Sloan Kettering for another difficult week of chemo. Or, I could view Nick's chemo—the last round scheduled for a while—as a bag of miracles. As toxic as they were, we held on to hope that they would wipe out more of those deadly cells and bring him closer to the three most beautiful letters in the alphabet: NED, or No Evidence of Disease.

I could have faith that 2006 would be the year that brought Nick to remission. I could walk through each day with the belief that Nick would survive and live a life rich with blessings. I could live 2006 with intention.

Spending the week at home with Nick definitely helped my attitude. It reminded me that, despite the war going on inside of him, my son was really just a sixteen-year-old kid. His week was filled with eating, four-wheeling, going to movies, playing video games, hanging out with friends, and spending a lot of time just enjoying being home, in his house. Now, as we prepared to plunge back into the day-to-day suffering of chemo, I prayed for the ability to hold on to my image of that "regular kid" and remember that the suffering would be temporary. Nick would bounce back and prevail. He would grow his hair back, put on weight, and get stronger.

I knew he was in the best possible hands at Sloan Kettering and was being carried by the spiritual hands of God.

With that combination, it just had to be a year of miracles and joy.

Chit Chat and Patience

After a week of hard treatment, Nick and I had gone to the clinic to get some extra fluids. In the waiting room, I tried to pass the time like I usually do, with some idle conversation. Nick was wiped out, but still managed to open one eye, crack a half-smile and say, "Mom, you need your girlfriends. I am really not listening to you."

Even after a punishing week, he was still my funny, wisecracking boy.

It was hard to believe I was entering my sixth month of dealing with the horror of a child with cancer, although, I had to admit, I was getting a lot better at it. Back in July and August, I couldn't even look at my son's scan reports without shaking and crying. Now I just read them matter-of-factly, knowing they were simply a snapshot of where we were at the moment and where we needed to go to get Nick to remission. Was this taking a toll on all of us? Of course. While Nick was making steady progress and all the news from the medical team had been good, it was exhausting to have medical jargon become our primary form of communication almost *all* the time. I was thankful for the unspoken language of our family's unity and love, and for any words that did not involve anti-nausea drugs or white cell counts. The slivers of time we talked about Nick returning to school, our granddaughter being potty trained, our son's recital at college...these slivers became escapes that nourished us and helped balance the rocking ship we were on.

I learned to stay flexible and open minded. I learned to have trust in a process I was totally unfamiliar with. I learned to remain optimistic and faithful that we were on the right path. And when the tears came—and they did often, and easily—I wiped them away and kept moving forward, with a laser focus on one mission: saving Nick's life.

A Week of Home Is Just What the Spirit Needs

One morning, while sitting in the clinic with my son, I saw a family reeling from the horror of the worst possible news. Doctors had just told them that nothing more could be done for their adorable, curly haired boy. Just hours later, Nick and I were back in Northern Virginia, where life was moving as if we never left. Images seared in my heart from that moment in clinic were locked away. It is how I coped, it is how I could keep my two worlds from colliding. I thought that must be what it felt like to be a soldier at war who suddenly gets an

R & R break. You're supposed to enjoy the gift of a few days of freedom to kick up your heels and enjoy life. But the images that have been etched in your mind don't go away. They are always there.

Still, being home with Nick was always a gift. He rested, ate, and visited with friends and family. He was always stronger and had more color in his face when he was home. Walking through our house, the walls were filled with pictures taken throughout his childhood. I hardly recognized the Nick I saw in those pictures—his pudgy cheeks, his braces, his carefree smile. He had grown into a man. He was old beyond his years and he had a wisdom that few will ever know.

The week raced by, culminating in a magical Saturday. While it was still January, the sun had a warmth that gave off a hint of spring. I looked down in our pasture and smiled as Nick threw the football with his brother and uncle, and my granddaughter and nephew petted the horses through the fence next door. Later, I laughed as Nick gave his grandparents a ride on his four-wheeler, and a huge smile spread across his face. I sat on my porch swing thinking, *This is life*. Pushing the little ones on the tree swing, rolling down the hill in the grass, walking around the pond, exploring the treasures of the barn...the day was a gift. That night, we celebrated with a cookout and a bonfire under the stars.

Life is a series of days, linked together by the people who share them with you. Nick's experiences at home played like a movie in his head when he was back in New York. Those days were also his life, as much as the battle that he endured. As we braced ourselves for the inevitable return to New York, I found comfort in the knowledge that those memories would sustain us as we felt the isolation and loneliness that treatment brought. I also knew that over the next few months, as spring returned, we would be able to return to Virginia more often to soak up the wonder of home. That gave us something to look forward to.

Taxi Cab Seats and Routines

Sometimes, the ride back to New York on the train was silent. Sometimes we all—Nick, Jim, and I—knew we had to "just do it." That meant staying focused, staying positive, and marching forward, doing what needed to be done. That night, as we got further from Virginia, I felt an eerie calm come over me. I knew that we were returning to our mission. We were going to eradicate whatever cancer remained in Nick's bone marrow. That was the only thing that mattered.

We arrived in the city just before ten at night and closed down the pizza place at the train station. The station was quiet and the streets rainy and dark. I thought to myself how far we had come. If anyone had told me a year before that I would be totally comfortable arriving late at night in a dark, rainy city, I would have said, "Not me!" But sitting down on the hard, crinkled leather seats of the New York taxi felt familiar and not at all scary.

We had all grown in ways we never imagined we would have to, and we were all stronger for it.

The most powerful tools that helped me cope with the massive changes to my life were my rituals and routines. I was trying so desperately to function in the cancer world. I needed things that were set in place so there was normalcy, a sense of security in the midst of the chaos. Settling in for nightly TV; walking to the corner for coffee and a paper; setting up my computer in the day hospital; watching *The Price is Right* with Nick at eleven every day; recording his blood counts in my day planner—these little things became the routine that gave structure to the long days and lonely nights. The repetition helped me feel safe. And as the rain came down on that last day of January 2006, I believed in my heart that everything would be okay.

A New York Weekend—Our World

When you're struggling to get through an extended crisis, so much of your energy is spent just trying to maintain your equilibrium. You never know when something might hit you out of the blue and cause all the emotion you're holding back to come bubbling to the surface. For Jim and me, that "something" turned out to be the movie *Walk the Line*.

We were hoping for a nice Sunday escape, just the two of us. We walked to the theater in the rain, sharing an umbrella and feeling cozy and happy. We munched popcorn and relaxed and thoroughly enjoyed the movie. And then, when it was over, we turned to look at each other—inexplicably we both started sobbing.

We were overcome with the realization that we had escaped room 309, the room the three of us shared, for a snuggly, romantic date. We felt confused, guilty, and out of place. We weren't in Virginia at our local multiplex. We hadn't seen a movie since this whole ordeal started the previous summer. Now, the fact that we were seeing a movie in New York City, and all the awful things that happened to get us there, overwhelmed us.

The rain had turned to bright daylight as we walked out of the theater. It brought us back to reality. We each took a deep breath and accepted that it was just one of *those* moments. We hurried back to Nick—to our son—and went into what I can only describe as a cave-like experience. We pulled the curtains on that Saturday afternoon and binge watched TV until midnight. We paused for spaghetti and ice cream, but that was about it. It was a very different kind of escape, together, as a family.

That night after we'd all gone to sleep, Nick got very sick. Jim had to leave the next morning, and the time came for him to go while Nick was still struggling in the bathroom. I took a break from helping Nick to say good-bye to my husband. I found him on his knees, praying. I knew it tore his heart out to leave us like that. But, I also knew that Nick and I would keep on, entering another week with our hearts filled with hope.

Blizzards and Nosebleeds

That final round of chemo proved to be tough. Nick's body was worn out to the point where he was no longer recovering as well. Then on day eleven, just like clockwork, the fever hit. We started February back on the inpatient side of the ninth floor. One night, while the threat of a huge snowstorm loomed on the horizon, we tucked into bed in our hospital room, anticipating a quiet night of sleep. That was not to be. Instead, Nick threw up, which triggered another epic nosebleed. Within minutes, we realized it wasn't going to stop; it just kept dripping like a faucet in desperate need of a plumber.

From the last nosebleed we had learned not to put his head back, but to lean forward. What we failed to realize was that the blood that would normally go down his throat was going to come out of his mouth! He almost filled a paper cup with it.

An ENT doctor joined us and told Nick he wanted him to blow his nose as hard as he could to clear the clot. Nick blew. His face turned bright red, the veins popped out. Suddenly, he expelled a three-inch clot and muttered, "I just gave birth."

Everyone laughed and said, "Yeah...it's a boy!"

This had become Nick's "signature"—trying to lighten the intensity of a tough situation with a one liner.

The nosebleed was severe enough to require Nick to stay a few more nights in the hospital. As sad and sick as he was, he still had a bit of childlike excitement, anticipating the snow that was scheduled to arrive. If we were at home in Virginia, we would have built a fire and snuggled up to watch a movie. Instead, we looked out at the snow falling through beams of light from the Queensboro Bridge, from our hospital room in New York. The next day, we watched the Olympics and marked another day off the calendar, bringing us one day closer to looking out our own windows on a pond, a big red barn, and horses in the field.

Valentine's Day

When I was a kindergarten teacher, Valentine's Day was by far the most exciting day of the year. As a young mother, I remember my own children laboring over the valentines for their classmates, making sure not to give a mushy one to the wrong child.

This was a different kind of Valentine's Day.

I set a small, red box of chocolates on Nick's blanket as he slept. A nurse technician named "Cowboy Jack" came in around seven thirty to take his vital signs. Nick was half asleep, but as Jack was leaving, he said, "Happy Valentine's Day, Jack." Jack looked surprised and gave Nick the biggest grin, saying "Happy Valentine's Day to you too, buddy." After he left, Nick looked at me and said, "I love to make people happy."

Then he went back to sleep.

The day clinic held a big Valentine's party. All the little kids from the inpatient side shuffled over with their IV poles and smiles. They decorated valentines, ate cupcakes, and watched a magic show. That was too much activity for Nick, so he stayed behind in his room. That's where he was when he received a visit from a seventeen-year-old boy named Michael.

Michael was also a cancer patient, and it turned out his Make-A-Wish wish was to come back to the hospital on Valentine's Day and hand out the most high-tech, expensive toys on the market to all the kids who were stuck there for the holiday.

Now, Nick had a *lot* of stuff. I was sure he would just say, "That's okay, I don't really need anything." But Michael held up something Nick definitely did *not* have—a video iPod, plus a card to buy some video downloads to watch on it. Nick beamed as he accepted this very extravagant and undeniably cool gift.

A few minutes after Michael left, he returned with a TV camera crew. New York's local Channel 11 was doing a story on kids with cancer and Michael's Make-A-Wish. This meant Nick was going to be on TV. After all the hoopla was over, Nick looked at me and said, "Now I know what I really want to do with my Make-A-Wish. I like making people feel happy, so I'm going to do something similar to what Michael did." He told me that we could still take a trip with our family somewhere as a regular family vacation, but he wanted his wish to be about something really meaningful. For him, that meant doing something to make other people happy.

I was so proud and touched.

The next night, February 15, Nick had his fifteen seconds of fame. I have to say it was surreal to see my son portrayed as the "cancer patient" on TV. How many times had I watched those clips with sadness for those poor kids and families? Now *that poor family* was us, watching our own lives play out on the ten o'clock news. Definitely another first, and definitely a very different Valentine's Day.

The Conductor

Nick continued to struggle to recover from that final round of chemo. Instead of bouncing back and getting stronger, he got feverish and very ill. Then the medical line that went into his chest got infected. He had been counting the days before he could get out of there and head home. Instead, we once again adjusted our compasses and settled in for what proved to be the longest hospital stay yet. But, there was a bright side. We were able to get Nick's scans and biopsies done while he was there being treated with massive doses of IV antibiotics. Finally we were discharged and went back to the Ronald McDonald House.

As always, waiting for scan and biopsy results was agonizing. They forgot to schedule Nick's echocardiogram, so we had to go back to the hospital the very next day. But when I wheeled Nick in and we chatted with our team, we finally got some good news. There was nothing more to do until Tuesday afternoon—and they thought Nick was strong enough to go home for the weekend.

Nick got a surge of energy, his smile returned, and we whipped into action. Jim had been with us and was getting ready to head back to Virginia to work. Happily, we added another suitcase to the pile. I felt completely frazzled, packing the IV pole, the bags of antibiotics, the tubing, the flushes of saline and heparin. It looked like a field hospital bag, but somehow, we made it out and got across the city in time to jump on the five-thirty train home.

We were so lucky. We happened to get on the train first and grab a set of four seats arranged facing each other like a booth. Jim and I sat down on one side, and Nick spread out on the two seats across from us so he could rest. But the train got very full, and pretty soon the conductor came over and asked Nick to sit up so someone could use the other seat. We explained our situation and he kindly put a ticket above that seat to say it was taken, even though we didn't pay for it. An hour later, he came back and told us a recliner seat had opened up in business class and offered to move us at no charge, but Nick was sleeping and didn't want to move. Still, it had been so sweet of the conductor to offer. Later, he tried to get a golf cart to take us from the train into Union Station in DC. By then Nick was rested and felt strong enough to walk, even though his bone-marrow sites were still really sore.

There were so many moments when I was moved by people's extra effort to make life a little more tolerable for us. *Sometimes even a smile instead of a stare gave me the strength I needed to navigate the next hour.*

A Knock on the Door

Back home in Virginia, awaiting the results of his latest scan, Nick received a surprise visitor. He opened the front door to see the head of Camp Varsity, his beloved summer camp, standing behind it. He and Nick embraced, and he handed Nick a letter inviting him back to camp that coming summer to serve as a counselor-in-training.

Nick had dreamed of being a counselor at Camp Varsity since his first summer there. His camp family had become like a second family to him, and becoming a counselor was both a privilege and a rite of passage. The administrators had agreed to let Nick work on a flexible schedule, whenever he was able.

This gave Nick a new goal, a new plan, and something to fill his mind with during the long weeks of waiting. His scan results had shown the tiniest bit of bone-marrow involvement, so he would need a few more weeks of lower-dose chemo before the start of the next treatment in his protocol. After months of setting tiny, daily goals, Nick now had a larger goal to accomplish.

As winter ended, signs of spring hinted that a summer of hope was on the way.

Parents' Night In

By this time, I had become somewhat of a "house mom" for many of the younger mothers at the "House." Kitchen talk, elevator chatter, and hugs in the lobby solidified bonds and created lifelong friendships. We craved our homes, our routines, and our other lives, but at least we had each other.

One night, a group of us gathered—without the kids—to share some drinks (usually forbidden) and appetizers. It turned into a real venting session, each mom or dad sharing stories, horrors and milestones that only those in our exclusive "club" could possibly understand. We all agreed that no one, in their wildest dreams, could really understand what it was like to live in a strange city, in a Ronald McDonald House, for months on end.

I shared a story about a recent trip I had taken with a bunch of families to an ice rink in the city. Nick had reluctantly agreed to go. Riding back I was sitting in the first row of seats in the van—there were about ten of us, several adults, several screaming kids, and Nick. At one point, I kind of spaced out and looked at myself from the outside. I was struck with an overwhelming feeling: "What the hell am I doing here? This is not my life, this is what happens to other people!" I snapped back to reality just as the van pulled back up to the Ronald McDonald House. I filed out with the rest of the residents, none of whom believed they would ever be in such a situation, all trying to make the best of it. That evening, talking and sharing a couple of beers with other parents was a welcome relief. In my bizarre, surreal world, it was a good Saturday night out, even if I only got as far as the second floor dining room.

The next morning, I woke up and walked to the corner to get coffee. Overnight, the trees along the street had burst into bloom. The glass barrier that protected the corner market from winter was down, and buckets of fresh flowers lined the street. The bleak, gray blanket of winter seemed to lift. I had the feeling that all of this was a fanfare, just for us, from nature.

New life was everywhere.

III
Antibody Treatment and NED

The Compass Point of Faith
What is our purpose on earth if not to embrace one another through hardship and help lighten the burdens that challenge our faith? The word "faith" is at the center of the compass on the tattoo. It reminds us to stay centered, as friends help carry us through darkness where faith is challenged and hope is hard to find.

After eight months spent enduring the highest dose chemotherapy a body can possibly handle, Nick was finally eligible to start the treatment that had brought us to Sloan Kettering in the first place—a Phase Two clinical trial using monoclonal antibodies.

The statistics on this new treatment were encouraging, with a long-term survival rate that was much more promising than the traditional protocol. The challenge was that the treatment would be extremely painful. Neuroblastoma is a nerve cell tumor, so the treatment would focus on the nerves of Nick's body, causing pain so intense he would need to be medicated with strong narcotics on each day of treatment. He would also need to inject a white blood cell stimulator, known as GMCSF, beginning a few days before treatment started, and again each day during the treatment.

Ideally, patients enter this phase with no disease evident. Nick still had two bone-marrow aspirates showing microscopic amounts of disease. However, since the antibodies used in treatment were known to kill microscopic marrow disease, we anticipated our next miracle.

The Lake

A week before we were due back at Sloan Kettering, we decided to enjoy some time away as a family, at our lake house. Nick started taking his GMCSF shots while we were there. It was yet another surreal experience to open the lake house refrigerator and see the vials of GMCSF sitting beside the yogurt, bagels, and orange juice. Still, I felt myself crossing over again, back to more normal things, the beat of normal life, with medical issues providing a counter-tempo. After eight months of living in New York and visiting home, our social worker had told us to expect the opposite—we would start to feel like we were visiting New York and living at home, which was an incredibly welcome change.

As we lay in bed one night, Jim asked me if I ever wondered what Nick thought about when he was alone. It occurred to me that Nick had not really had much time by himself since his whole ordeal started. At the Ronald McDonald House, our beds were less than two feet apart. In the hospital, my chair bed was right up against his. Even when we were home, his friends usually spent the night with him.

As we talked, we realized Nick was still up, watching TV. Jim got up and joined him, and they stayed up until midnight, just hanging out and talking. We were in a great place that week at the lake. We were hopeful. Nick's test results were almost clean, and a miraculous new treatment was around the corner. But we knew that there would be tough times ahead. We adopted a true carpe diem mentality. We tried to seize every day that was good and enjoy even the smallest moments together. Those became our new memories to hold on to.

The summer before, the lake had been a place of anguish and worry. It was where we went for breaks during all of Nick's testing. It was a place of a lot of bleak discussions, all held under that dark cloud that kept closing in on us. That morning, as Nick jabbed his thigh with one more GMCSF shot, we hoped that this summer we would make new and beautiful memories at the lake together. We already had many from that week to add to our "bank"—Jim and Nick fishing and catching three bass, Nick playing cards with his sister, doing watercolor painting with Alexis, hanging out on the dock, driving the boat. We left feeling fortified to face the week ahead, whatever it might hold.

Eight Hundred Bees

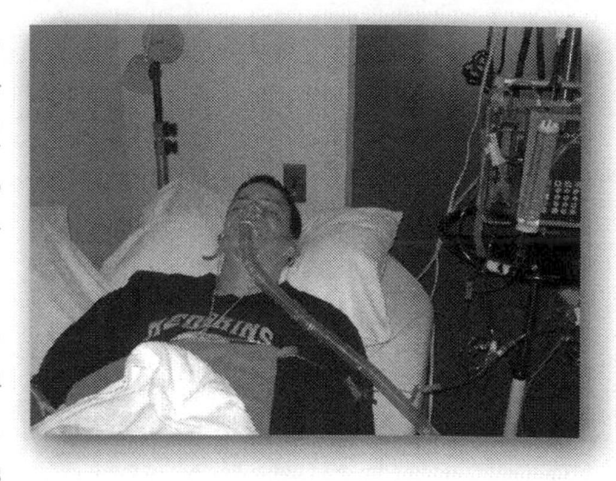

When Nick arrived for his first antibody treatment, we were all very worked up and tense. How painful would it be? Would Nick be able to handle it? There was no way to know in advance.

When the antibody drip started, Nick pulled his stocking cap down over his eyes and turned up his iPod. Ten minutes later, his stomach was the first spot to feel the pain. He said it felt like eight hundred bees were stinging his body, complete with the throbbing that persists after the sting is over. Soon the stings were spreading—to his legs, then his back, then his arms, then his hands. Through it all, Nick coped, using oxygen, deep breathing, and moaning. The doctors were pleased—apparently, the fact that Nick was hurting meant that the infusion was working.

The infusion of drugs only lasted for about an hour, but the residual pain was so intense we couldn't just get up and go home. For the next four hours Nick needed ice packs, heat packs, massages, and lots of dilaudid—a strong painkiller. Then, after all of that, he kind of came to and said, "That wasn't as bad as I thought it would be. I didn't cuss, and I didn't cry."

I laughed. But mostly, I felt so proud of him.

The pain from antibody treatment never really went away. That first night, Nick was still hurting and needed strong pain medication. I remember him trying so hard to watch TV and stay awake with us, but his eyes just wouldn't stay open. We were all drained and exhausted, but somewhat relieved that we were no longer facing the unknown of antibody treatment. We now knew what to expect. We knew Nick could weather this important step with bravery and strength.

Then suddenly, Nick awakened from his sleep and told us,

"I couldn't do any of this stuff without you two…you are my life support machine…don't come unplugged."

A Road Trip, a Plane Trip, and Family Reunited

After eight months of living in room 309 at the Ronald McDonald House, we drove south down Route 95 with our mission accomplished. Antibody therapy was two weeks on, followed by two weeks off. In our world, two weeks off was a very, very big deal. Two weeks feels like two months in "cancer time." We had learned to cherish each moment that we didn't have a medical inconvenience to deal with.

While Nick was going through treatment, our oldest son, Jeff, was pursuing a music performance major at the Indiana University School of Music. He constantly worried about his little brother; it had often been difficult for him to stay focused. By chance, Jeff's first solo recital was scheduled for the weekend after Nick's first round of antibodies, and there was absolutely no way Nick was going to miss it. He was determined to fight through the residual pain and make the trip back to Virginia, and then to Indiana, all in twelve hours.

After unloading the car in Virginia, pulling out the things we needed to pack for the trip to Indiana, we finally fell into bed. The next day, we managed to get eleven people to the airport and connect with two more there. Once we reached Indiana, seeing Jeff and feeling the intense connection of our family circle, made all the stress and effort of getting there worth it. The weekend was fabulous and Jeff's recital breathtaking, especially his two original compositions, which were very moving to me. The second piece, which he named "December," was written for Nick, who was born in December. Jeff was overcome by emotion when explaining the music to the audience and had to leave the stage for a moment to regain his composure.

There were moments that weekend when I almost forgot that we weren't just like other families. There were moments when I thought, *Can't this just be over now? Haven't we paid our dues?* But most moments I was painfully aware of who we were, and what our situation was. We were a strong family that had been dealt a really crappy hand. It took all of our strength, and all of our energy, to function in the normal world. *We strove to keep our family going in the right direction emotionally, mentally, and physically. It was incredibly hard, but worth it. We worked hard every day to see good in every day.*

That day in Indiana our family felt the goodness of the day, and so much more.

Walking Side by Side, Miracles in the Making

During that summer in 2005 when our nightmare began, Nick's second cousin, Tommy, also experienced a health crisis. At just twenty-five years old, he was paralyzed wrestling around with friends. He was told there was not much hope for any body movement from the shoulders down. Tommy wouldn't accept that. During the year that followed, Tommy not only shocked the entire medical community with his progress; he was part of a miracle. In that way, he had something in common with Nick.

One year after his accident, his church held the first annual "Tommy Walks 5k." When Nick heard that Tommy was planning to walk, he was determined to muster up the strength to join him. Nick walked side by side with Tommy and his steel crutches, never leaving his cousin's side. He pushed forward to see how much of the walk he could do. Tommy had not been a cousin Nick even knew that well, but the bond that they shared on that walk brought tears to my eyes. I saw human determination and medical expertise partner with God's power. Two miracles walked down the streets of small-town America inspiring onlookers. It was a true demonstration of faith in action.

Caryn Franca

Not Your Typical Conversation between Two Teens

The weather grew warmer and signs of spring splashed onto the canvas of our life. We returned to New York for some testing after the first round of antibodies.

While waiting to be put to sleep for a bone marrow biopsy, Nick struck up a conversation with another young patient. A week before, the young man had been preparing for his freshman exams at Penn State, winding down his first year in their golf management program. He went to the school clinic thinking he was run down and maybe had mono. Now, a week later, he was at Sloan Kettering diagnosed with leukemia. That's how he spent exam week of his freshman year. He had a job lined up to teach golf over the summer, instead he would be enduring chemo. That's how quickly life can change.

The poor kid was nervous, having never been under anesthesia before. Nick was just like a wise old man, telling him it was "awesome" when they gave you the white milky stuff (Propofol) because it only lasted a little while. Nick was so matter of fact about it, so at ease with the process, that I am sure it eased the new boy's mind. It's another one of those moments that will be frozen in my memory forever—two teenage boys' normal teenage conversation about a subject no teen should ever have to talk about.

But that was normal now, just like the process of flying to New York, having a surgical procedure, and returning home to Virginia the same day. Once, I would have thought that was impossible, but that's exactly how we spent that day. We flew to New York, Nick had bone marrow sucked out from his hips, and by seven-thirty that night, he was back home in Virginia. The four bandages on his hips were the only evidence of New York, as he enjoyed the sunset with his dad and a fishing pole.

Make the most of each day, right?

He yelled up for me to look down at the pond, beaming as he held up a decent-sized bass. Then, just the way his grandfather taught him, he kissed the fish and released it back into the water—and to life.

May 1, 2006 NED

It was six-thirty in the evening, just one day after Nick's bone marrow biopsy, when my phone rang. I looked at the caller ID and saw a number with a 212 area code. New York City. My heart stopped. Bone-marrow results take days to get back. I wondered, *What could be wrong?*

Dr. Kushner was on the line, and thankfully, he didn't make me wait to find out. Immediately, he said, "All bone marrow is negative for neuroblastoma!"

Less than a year after Nick's ordeal began, we had reached that magical state called NED—No Evidence of Disease.

Dr. Kushner explained that Nick would continue to receive the painful antibody treatments every two weeks for up to two years, or until his body developed a resistance to them. But in between his regular visits, he would be able to resume a normal life, which included returning to high school in the fall.

That was definitely something to look forward to.

A Fist Pump through the Pain

Sometimes, the residual pain caused by the antibody treatment was more than Nick could bear. I remember one day, early in treatment, when, no matter what we did, Nick couldn't get relief. For an hour and a half, we massaged him, put ice packs and heat packs on him, and helped him with oxygen and breathing. But even with the maximum amount of narcotics in his system, he couldn't get enough relief to go to sleep. In the midst of that, Dr. Kushner suddenly popped his head in. Nick opened his eyes, held out his hand and simply said, "Dr. Kushner"—as in, "help me."

For the next thirty minutes, Dr. Kushner stood by Nick's bed and held the oxygen for him. He calmed him down, assuring him that his vitals were perfect and he was doing a good job. Nick opened his eyes, looked at the doctor and said, "Thank you so much." He then held his fist up to the doctor and said, "rock." Usually when Nick did that, the other person would tap their fist back, a gesture of unity and friendship. Well...I don't think Dr. Kushner had ever done a "rock" before. He asked if it was "a Southern thing." He quickly learned how to do it, and the fist-to-fist connection made Nick smile. A couple of tears snuck out of my eyes as I watched a world-famous researcher and oncologist take that time to be with my son.

HIPAA!

Chemotherapy is intended to destroy bad cells. Antibody treatment is designed to build the immune system back up after chemo destroys it. That was hard to remember when the treatment to accomplish that goal was so agonizing. The parents nicknamed the block of rooms where the antibody treatments were infused the "House of Pain." It was truly bizarre to witness parents and their heroic children dutifully returning for more of the same torment, day after day. But somehow, we all did it. We had no choice. This was the best treatment available. We wanted our children to have a fighting chance. So, we kept going back for more.

One especially hard day, Nick held on until the end of the drip, but then, suddenly, he felt like he could not breathe. When he tried to talk, nothing came out. We had to put an oxygen mask on him, as opposed to just the hose, which was the normal procedure, and he got very angry with me! I couldn't understand what he was saying, until finally, he managed to say what he had been struggling to say...

"You suck at this, Mom."

Of course, he apologized when he felt better. This was all part of our newest new normal. Pain here, pain there, breathing challenges...the usual.

After the infusion, Nick would sleep it off for a few hours, and sometimes the nurses would come by to chat. That day, two of the nurse practitioners who were very close to Nick stopped in. They were joking around and telling funny Nick stories when Nick suddenly yelled from his oxygen mask, "HIPAA!" In hospital speak, that meant the nurses were not supposed to be talking about him without his consent. Once again, through exhaustion and pain, Nick found a way to lighten the mood. Everyone laughed, and then each nurse took a leg and massaged him for a good ten minutes. He smiled letting them massage away some of the day's pain.

Hot Coals and Yo-Yo's

After another brutal morning of treatment another afternoon was spent sleeping it off in the "House of Pain." It was another bizarre, but comforting ritual we had created. As five-thirty approached, he finally woke up. Once again, he insisted on walking back to the Ronald McDonald House. He looked like he was walking on hot coals the whole way home. Up ahead of us, a mother walked with her three daughters. They were skipping and laughing and playing with a yo-yo. Nick commented, "Look at them, not a care in the world, having fun. Who knows—they could have a tumor growing inside of them." At one point, when we were waiting to cross the street, I noticed his legs shaking in pain. But he just kept putting one foot in front of the other, like he always did.

I was so proud of him.

Being Santa

The weekend in the middle of Nick's two-week antibody treatments was a godsend. Those two days off gave his body a break from the excruciating pain and allowed him to recover a little bit and rest up for the next week. He was even able to eat a few good meals. We went back to the clinic late Monday morning, Nick felt recharged and ready—or as ready as a person could be to endure another week of unbearable pain.

While we waited (longer than usual, because it was Monday), we bumped into a young mother with a beautiful little two-year-old boy we had met a few months before. Nick had fallen in love with the little boy, who also had neuroblastoma. The young mom could have easily been my daughter. She told us some of her story and I was so impressed by her choices. Just twenty-one, but she had dedicated herself to being a good mother to her two-year-old, despite being single and lonely. She did everything right during her pregnancy and as a parent, but here she was in Cancer World.

It turned out this young woman and her son had just moved right across the hall from us at the "House." We ended up walking back together after treatment. The little boy wanted his mommy to carry him because he was in pain, so Nick volunteered to push the empty stroller, which gave him something to lean on and helped his own pain. Later, Nick babysat the boy while the two moms went down to the dining hall for dinner.

That night, as Nick and I stared at the ceiling waiting for sleep to take us away, he had an idea. He remarked that our family "had so much," and he thought it would be cool to surprise the young mom with "a check in an envelope under her door." I was so moved. I called home to run it by Jim, who said yes immediately. Nick was stoked as I wrote a four-digit check and slid it under her door, like Santa Claus, late at night. My son went to sleep in pain, but with a smile on his face. The rest of that week of treatment was tough, but by focusing on this other family and the gift of being able to offer them some comfort, Nick was also comforted.

Reaching out of your own pain to help others can be a powerful part of healing.

Two Weeks at Home: Shingles, a New Nephew, Golf Clubs, and Fishing Poles

We had been home for just a few hours after completing another two-week antibody cycle when Nick started complaining about something in his eye. The diagnosis was aggressive shingles. Because cancer treatment had hit Nick's immune system so hard, he was especially susceptible to this disease, which typically affects older people. Now, with only two precious weeks to spend at home, we wound up in isolation at the local hospital.

Nick was in extreme pain and was feeling depressed and very down. We had planned to go out with his great buddy Michael and his family to celebrate Michael's high school graduation. Instead, Michael and his family brought carry out food to his isolation room. We celebrated Michael's graduation in matching yellow isolation gowns. Michael said he wouldn't have it any other way.

Meanwhile, we continued to wait on the arrival of my daughter's second baby. My mental state was so fragmented. Nick's shingles put me back in that familiar tunnel where I could only focus on one step at a time. Nothing could be planned. But Nick was determined to make it home for the baby's arrival, and that wish was granted.

Home from the hospital and on the mend, Nick was able to meet his new nephew before our "break" from New York was over. It was a day of very mixed emotions for me. Seeing a precious new member of our family reminded me of how perfectly healthy Nick was for so long. I could not help but feel a pang of sadness along with the joy I was experiencing. After the celebration of seeing his nephew, Nick was able to join his crowd of beautiful, supportive friends at a graduation cookout and things became crystal clear again. *I chose gratitude for how far we had come, and not the obstacles in getting there.*

With only a few days left at home, it did my heart good to see Nick pull out of the driveway in his cousin's car with golf clubs and fishing poles. They had decided to head to the lake on a mini road trip. On the way, they stopped at Nick's summer camp, where they visited with all of his amazing supporters. After a day at our lake house, they stopped to visit my parents and watch fireworks. Nick and his cousin spent the night there and then came home. We headed back to New York the very next day.

Two weeks at home. In true Nick fashion, he went from shingles and hospitalization to celebrating the joy of meeting his new nephew—not to mention a road trip. We headed back to our other world filled with more good memories.

A Different Kind of Fourth of July

Nick and Michael, Fourth of July at the Ronald McDonald House

There is really no other earthly experience that I can imagine—besides war, maybe—that rivals the battle that is the world of cancer. Nick's friend, Michael, decided to come back to New York with us for the week so Nick wouldn't feel left out on the fourth of July that weekend. He sat with us as Nick's first infusion of antibodies began, and the contrast between the two friends was heartbreaking. There was Michael, still in the real world, and Nick, beginning to slip from that world, into his daily world of pain. It was so damned sad.

Michael was quiet and helpful, applying hot packs and sitting by Nick's side. Nick needed a ton of drugs to endure the pain, so he slept in the clinic until six-thirty and fell back asleep as soon as we got back to the "House." He kept trying to wake up to be some company for Michael. He tried to eat some pasta, but kept drifting off to sleep midchew. Through it all, Michael sat patiently, just loving and supporting his friend.

As the week wore on, Michael started to get the hang of the daily treatment routine. At night, he'd watch TV with Nick as the pain and drugs from the treatment wore off. One night, with the Fourth of July coming up, footage of the previous year's annual Nathan's Hot Dog Eating contest came on. The boys decided that, since they were in New York, and since the contest was on Saturday, we should all head out to Coney Island to see it live.

Well, who was I to squash the excitement of two boys who wanted to watch grown men consume way too much processed meat? Before I knew it, I had booked a car service to pick us up Saturday morning and take us to Coney Island.

It was all so "New York," entering the black town car and exiting "Cancer World," even for just a little while. Nick was in some pain from the long week of treatments, but the adventure took his mind off his situation. Soon we had blended in with forty-thousand people standing shoulder to shoulder, and watched the winner eat fifty-three hot dogs in twelve minutes. The sun was hot and Nick was tired, but none of that stopped him from smiling and cheering and embracing the day.

Crossing back over onto East Seventy-Third Street, we all were pretty proud that we pulled that road trip off, and we weren't even done. After a nap, we headed out again, boarding the police bus that took the Ronald residents to a cookout and fireworks at a park on the East River. While it was definitely a party no one wants to be invited to—a Families with Cancer Party—the setting was still pretty incredible, and it was still a lot of fun. Gathered all together, we didn't really see the bald heads, backpacks of fluids, and wheelchairs. We were all just parents and children celebrating the Fourth of July on the river in New York City. It was a nice day. The next day, Michael went home, and Nick returned to the "House of Pain."

Freddie

After sending Michael to the train station in a cab, Nick and I arrived at the clinic midmorning. As usual, Nick's pain during treatment was intense, but he tried hard to breathe through it and make it through with less medication. His little buddy was in the clinic, and Nick woke up long enough to play some peekaboo and make him laugh.

On our walk home, I stopped at the grocery store. Nick kept walking toward the "House." When I turned the corner, groceries in hand, I saw Nick still out on the street, talking to a semi–street person. There they were, deep in conversation about life and religion. The man was grateful that Nick reached out to him.

I was not entirely surprised; it was so Nick.

Later, when I asked Nick about it, he said a voice told him to reach out and talk to the guy. He said they talked for about ten minutes and that he never once felt awkward. As he drifted off to sleep, I heard him say, "Freddie…something changed in me today from that experience." We met so many angels during our journey, in so many shapes and sizes. Freddie was one of them.

Golf Balls and Happy Hour

We met another new family who was in New York getting treatment for their seventeen-year-old son. He was an amazing young man, and this is the part I couldn't help connecting to— he was a golfer, like Nick. I was so moved by this passage from his journal:

> *I went to the driving range the other day and I was thinking…*
>
> *I was thinking how you start out with a big bucket full of golf balls, and you just start hitting away carelessly. You have dozens of them, each individual ball means nothing so you just hit, hit, hit. One ball gone is practically inconsequential when subtracted from your bottomless bucket. There are no practice swings or technique re-evaluations after a bad shot, because so many more tries remain. Yet eventually you start to have to reach down towards the bottom of the bucket to scavenge for another shot and you realize that tries are running out. Now with just a handful left, each swing becomes more meaningful. The right technique becomes more crucial, so between each shot you take a couple practice swings and a few deep breaths. There is*

a very strong need to end on a good note, even if every preceding shot was horrible, getting it right at the end means a lot. You know as you tee up your last ball, "This is my final shot, I want to crush this with perfection; I must make this count." Limited quantities or limited time brings a new, precious value and significance to anything you do. Live every day shooting as if it's your last shot, I know I have to.
Miles Levin

We had parents' night out on the terrace outside my bedroom, and Miles's mother joined us. It was fun, despite the awful circumstances that brought us together. Getting to know all kinds of parents, from all over the world, was still an incredible experience. Their stories were sad, sometimes desperate, and sometimes hopeful. We all sat sharing a beer like it was happy hour in our own neighborhood back home except, in this new "neighborhood," we all had one common goal—to save our children's lives. That common bond made for fast friendships and a silent understanding.

Humble and Grateful

The first time I held out my plate and looked in the eyes of a stranger serving me dinner in the Ronald McDonald House dining hall, it was such an odd experience. I remember feeling so grateful to this stranger for taking the time to offer me a meal, but also feeling completely uncomfortable. For the first time in my adult life I was the one receiving instead of giving. It was a feeling I would eventually get used to. Through the years of our battle, the gestures of others would feed my body and nourish my soul.

One of those gestures still is vivid in my mind today. It was a visit from a crew of stylists from the Elizabeth Arden Red Door Salon, who set up shop in the Ronald McDonald House playroom. I got a haircut and a manicure. There were also massages and facials, plus wine, food, and even volunteers to help with the little ones while their moms enjoyed some long-needed pampering. The evening created an incredible sense of community. Smiles were shared among strangers and friends alike—smiles that needed no words. The transformation of tired, emotionally drained mamas was a joy for us all to share. That little window of self-care fed our spirits to face another day.

Friendship and Fishing

With the weekend approaching, Nick and I set off on a completely new adventure. We took the train north up the coast to Mystic, Connecticut. My dear friend from college lives on the water in Mystic, and she and her husband offered a weekend of relaxation and a little boating. Even though Nick was exhausted from another week in the "House of Pain," the idea of spending some time away from the city made his energy soar. So, of course, we made the trip.

The value of simple things in life is magnified when life as you knew it is stripped away. We boarded their little skiff and motored out to a beautiful calm area. Nick was so happy to be on the water. He threw in a line and settled in, soaking up the joy. After a while, he pulled in a decent sized flounder. He was the only one on the boat to catch anything.

After we were back on land, Nick looked at me and said, "I needed that, I really needed that Mom. Fishing just calms me down and relaxes me." Afterward, he borrowed my friend's bike and rode around the seaport town. No one who saw him had any idea of the struggle he lived every day, and the challenges he faced. Nor could they have understood how rare it was for him to just have the simple freedom to ride a bike. After he returned, he sat out on a second story deck with my friend's dog, gazing at the sun as it dropped below the horizon, completing a beautiful day.

That simple gesture to share their weekend with us, created immense gratitude and renewed energy.

Camp 2006: Achieving the Goal

Nick had been at his beloved summer camp, Camp Varsity, when his life was shattered.

He was there when he got that fateful phone call; when we had to pick him up immediately and take him home to have test after test, then surgery, then everything else that followed. Yes, he had to leave camp, but Nick's camp family was always with him. The outpouring of support received from them after his diagnosis did more than medicine to keep him going. Friends from camp visited him at Ronald McDonald House. When he was alone, when he was enduring his darkest days of treatment, he stared at pictures from camp and read and reread emails of encouragement from his friends.

Determined to not let his illness define who he was, he set a goal. Even though at the time he weighed just 115 pounds, he would get strong enough to go back the next summer and be a counselor in training, just like he always believed he would.

He talked about this goal with anyone who would listen. He planned and strategized what kind of medical support he might need. He even created a story for the very large scar covering his side from back to front. He planned to tell the kids that he had been attacked by a shark! For months, he lay in bed at night planning his return.

And one year after his ordeal began—on a day when the heat index in Central Virginia was 113—Nick achieved that goal.

With a few prescriptions, daily white cell boosting shots tucked into the camp nurse refrigerator and a few pounds gained, Nick was back to the place he loved. He worked as a counselor for the six- to eight-year-old boys, and lived in a small, wooden cabin with no air conditioning. For Nick this was actually an improvement over some of the places he had called "home" for the past year: a small room at the Ronald McDonald House he shared with me, hospital rooms he shared mostly with small children, and ICU rooms shared with multiple machines and monitors.

At Camp Varsity he created new memories—of outdoor games, rope swings into rivers, ghost stories, and fellowship around a fire. They were the memories that fed his soul and strengthened his friendships.

They were a normal kid's memories.

Hoodies and Carpool Lines

During that first long year, I couldn't have imagined Nick returning to high school. But, it was actually happening. The new school year was about to start. Nick went out with his cousin Greg to buy a new backpack and a notebook! He would be returning to the real world. I would be just another mom in the carpool line.

Rain was pouring down as I dropped Nick off for his first day back. He disappeared into the crowd of hooded sweatshirts and new backpacks. He looked just like every other kid walking into a new school year. I didn't get caught up in the emotion of the moment. I just reflected on how normal everything felt. No one knew how he would come and go, juggling high school with monthly trips to New York to endure more painful and exhausting treatments. No one knew that emotionally, this seemingly typical high-school boy had morphed into a man, and had experienced an entirely different kind of education. It would have been hard to explain, so why try? How could any of his peers grasp the hell he had gone through? They just saw him in the halls, smiling and being Nick.

Nick didn't turn back to look at me on that most auspicious "first day of school." He just walked through the doors to do what normal kids do every September. I turned on my blinker, merged out of the parking lot, and drove home with a smile, eyes filled with grateful tears and a heart filled with optimism.

Our New New-Normal

As Nick fell back into the normal cadence of the days and weeks of the school year, I found myself reflecting on the person my boy had become.

Facing cancer had made Nick a wiser, more tolerant person. He returned to school having seen and experienced pain and suffering his peers couldn't possibly imagine. He knew kids who had died. Through it all, he found strength within himself that most teenagers don't know they possess.

And yet, when he was outside that clinical, medical environment, he didn't dwell on it, or even talk about it. He was just Nick, in high school, doing his thing.

The weekend before our first trip back to New York for treatment was spent digging, planting, and building, helping his cousin Greg complete his Eagle Scout project. I had to drop his immune booster shots off at the work site in the morning because he had stayed there overnight. In his nonchalant manner, he walked away for a moment, climbed into the van, filled the syringe, jabbed himself in the thigh, limped around for a minute or two, and then got back to work.

We don't always know who among us is dealing with an illness or handicap. Most often, like with Nick, it's private, concealed like a secret. Wouldn't all of humanity be better served if we approached everyone with empathy and compassion?

Nick's illness taught me that every single person has their own story—and, most likely a significant part of their story I don't know. It is human nature to want to fit in and not draw attention to our differences. Today, I try harder to always be a little kinder than I used to be. I try to notice if someone is struggling. *I try not to judge if someone I meet is not easy to get along with. Burdens are hard to carry. You just never know what difficulty a person may be enduring.*

Most people who encountered Nick at this point in his life had no idea that this kid—this happy, normal kid—was actually battling a horrendous monster. They would only know if they happened to see the port in his chest, or a syringe, or the huge scars covering the front and back of his body. If that did happen, I hoped they would see those things as something he had to do, not something that defined him.

Back in New York

It was September 11, 2006. Five years had passed since our country was violated and thousands of innocent people, who were just doing their jobs or going about their lives, lost their lives. Cancer is like that. Innocent people are just living their lives and then, out of nowhere, often with no warning or preparation, they're instantly thrown into survival mode. Their vision becomes a tunnel; nothing else matters except to escape the burning building that is raging inside their body.

Nick was learning to navigate his own rescue from the assault. Throughout the fall and winter of 2006, he managed to move between school and treatment with a wisdom beyond his years.

Balloons

Back in New York, we met a little boy from South Africa who also had neuroblastoma. His doctors back home had told his family that there was not much that they could do for him. So his family left everything—including their continent—to see if Sloan Kettering could give them hope.

After a massive surgery and very high-dose chemotherapy, the little boy was finally allowed to return to the Ronald McDonald House. Mom and dad were pushing him in one stroller and his eighteen-month-old brother in another. His dad and mom were also pushing suitcases, blankets, diaper bags, and more down First Avenue. I was walking up to the hospital with Nick for his antibody treatment when we saw them and the mom spotted me. She said, "Oh Caryn, Connor is so sad we left his big balloons in the room at the hospital. When you come home today will you bring them back with you?" I was thrilled to do it. I knew how stressful getting out of the hospital, and settling back in at the Ronald was after surgery. Balloons…I could definitely help with that!

At five thirty that afternoon, I woke Nick up from a rough antibody day. He had a splitting headache and was in no mood for chitchat, but he put his game face on for the walk home. I almost forgot about the balloons, but remembered in time and walked over to the inpatient side to retrieve them.

It was a massive bunch of Spiderman and SpongeBob balloons, all tied together. Nick shook his head as he coped with his pain and I coped with a larger than life superhero bouquet, struggling to hold them up without bumping into anyone, or annoying Nick, as we walked down the street.

We were about a block from Ronald McDonald House when a little boy in a stroller saw the balloons and said to his mother,

"Oh, Mommy, they are going to a birthday party. Look at the balloons!"

It felt like a slap in the face. In the normal world, balloons are associated with parties. In our world, they give a child something to look at that is fun and happy, and a diversion from the monitors and IVs of a hospital room. They are a symbol of a triumphant step in the march against the disease. They bring smiles to children who have been robbed of things like pain free birthday parties and innocent celebrations.

I knocked on the door of room 805 and delivered Connor's balloons. I felt like an angel and a new friend all in one.

Every Little Thing Is Going to Be All Right

October 2006. We were back at the clinic for Nick's seventh round of antibody treatment—his second since returning to school. The contrast between clinic life and normal life hit us in the face. Within an hour of our arrival, I learned about a little girl who had just finished her first round of antibodies the week before. They did an MIBG scan (the same scan Nick was scheduled to receive that week) and discovered that the cancer was consuming her liver. She was inpatient, and they were trying to get her home. She wouldn't see Halloween.

We learned that another sixteen-year-old who we had become friendly with was now in the same situation. It took all our strength to focus on our mission that week.

So, we pulled up our courage, leaned on our faith, and swallowed hard. It was Monday morning, we were back in New York, and we weren't there for the big Columbus Day Parade. We had our own plans to march toward.

Luckily, our news was good that week. Nick's blood work was excellent and—more importantly—he got a really good report on a "special" test he had requested in September. He had his full immunity back, which meant it was now safe for him to do something that was very important to him, albeit a bit baffling to me.

He had decided to get a tattoo.

Dr. Kushner was not a fan of tattoos. At first, he actually tried to pretend Nick's number had to be higher than was actually necessary to dissuade him. But once Nick explained that he wanted the tattoo to commemorate his experience with cancer, the good doctor relented and shook his head with a smile.

Now, armed with this welcome news, Nick spent the entire week in between the pain of and recovery from antibody treatment, sketching multiple concepts of what would be his defining stamp on cancer—his tattoo. How could I not agree to sign the underage consent form? As I mused at his drawings I couldn't help but feel proud and elated that the designs he had created were all thoughtful and meaningful. There was not a single design that said, "Fuck You Cancer!"

Not that I would have blamed him.

Through it all, that Bob Marley song kept playing in my head—the one with the lyrics that say:

"Don't worry about a thing 'cause every little thing gonna be alright."

That was the way we chose to continue to live.

Trick or Treat

Happy Halloween. Whatever memories those words bring up for you, for me, they bring back the magic of dreaming and pretending and some of the best nights I have experienced as a mom. Our postcard town of historic homes completely transforms every Halloween, the streets filling with people and the air with magic. It is one of those unifying experiences that makes a hometown a place of love and security.

That Halloween, Nick got to be home. His goal was to get out of the house and onto the streets of his hometown to trick-or-treat with his niece and nephew. He wanted to blend in, as if his childhood had never been interrupted. As it turned out that wasn't easy. He stayed home from school that day with a bad nosebleed and extreme nausea. Still, with his goal set, he spent the day sleeping, trying to gather strength for the Halloween tradition, and he made it.

For me, as always, it was wonderful to be home. I saw so many friends, and waved and chatted as I walked those magical streets. But as I walked, suddenly, a shadow crept over me, more terrifying than any of the staged "scary" scenes around town. Our doctors in New York called and wanted to move Nick's quarterly scan up to the next week. They told me they were a little concerned about something.

How many times would I have to bounce between my two worlds in the course of one day? One minute I was looking at my beautiful, healthy almost-seventeen-year-old, and the next I was dreading tests and results that could literally change his chance for life in a heartbeat. As every mom dealing with cancer knows, the toll is cumulative. That bone tired weariness is always there, fighting to take over.

But that night I didn't let myself "go there." I tried to stay in the moment and concentrate on helping Nick feel well enough to enjoy the night. Afterward, I savored the memory of a perfect evening, filled with magic and fun. I thought of Nick with his niece on his shoulders, helping her learn the ropes of Halloween in his town. I thought of doors that opened to welcome new memories and old friends, who were so happy to see Nick.

Next week would arrive soon enough.

Back in New York, we were relieved when the "shadow" they saw was just that—a shadow, not cancer. We were cleared to receive more antibodies and less stress for me!

"We're all in this thing together, walking the line between faith and fear."—Old Crow Medicine Show

During an antibody treatment, those were the words Nick was listening to on his iPod. He handed me one of the earbuds. He told me it was a song he liked a lot and that they listened to it at camp. We listened together and I squeezed his hand as I looked in his eyes. It was one of those moments.

I felt very connected to my son as we listened together, even though he was slightly agitated because I had the earbud in upside down.

I felt a weird sense of peace that day in the "House of Pain," something I think we both shared. Every set of eyes I glanced at, every new family I mourned for, every child who cried out reminded me that we were all walking that line between faith and fear. The silent "knowing" provided a sense of common connection. Those of us who felt like we were in a balanced place on that line would reach out to those who were teetering. Over time, the many, many people who walked that line with us became the fiber that held our path together. With God overseeing the process, and angels on earth supporting us, we walked with more faith than fear...most of the time.

Forced Family Fun at the Tattoo Parlor where Courage, Strength, Family, Faith, and Friendship Became Our Emblem

Courage Friends Strength Family Faith

Thanksgiving arrived again. A year before, the whole family lined up to board a bus with the rest of the "House" residents to go see the balloons of the Macy's Day parade. This year, the big day had arrived. Nick wanted to celebrate Thanksgiving 2006 by finally getting his tattoo.

I'll admit this sounded a little crazy to me. After seven months of treatment in the "House of Pain," I didn't understand the upside of voluntarily having even more needles stuck into his flesh. But, Nick's doctors had given him the okay, and just like that, the most memorable incident of Forced Family Fun in Franca family history was about to take place!

"Forced Family Fun," or FFF, was our catch-all term for a supposedly fun event Jim and I dragged our kids to, often with great reluctance on their part. Over the years, the acronym was applied to everything from a family board game to an excursion to somewhere *we* thought would be educational. Our vision didn't always match their reaction! This particular FFF switched up the traditional FFF model because this time it was Nick and the kids dragging us off to participate in an activity they, specifically Nick, had chosen. I am pretty sure we would have never chosen this forced family fun adventure!

Nick chose to have his tattoo placed on his back between his shoulder blades. There was not an ounce of extra fat there to cushion the needles, and he felt every drip of ink being etched! He bit his cheek so hard from the pain that it almost bled. Each member of the family had their own encounter with the tattoo artist. A version of Nick's compass was inked onto a body part of their choosing. I decided to limit mine to the word "Faith" and had it tattooed on my lower back, exactly where Nick's tumor had been.

Who could have ever imagined a year before, that Nick would be getting a tattoo to represent his cancer journey? Who could have imagined an infant in a car seat hanging out at a tattoo parlor for three hours? Who could have imagined a toddler getting a fake tattoo to be a part of the party? The tattoo parlor FFF, together as a family, was one of the many unique and powerful ways Nick's cancer brought us together as a family—and resulted in an unforgettable Thanksgiving.

Another Birthday

As a baby, Nick was a cute, curly haired little guy. Being the third child, he was always taken care of by siblings, friends, family...always surrounded with love. None of us ever imagined that he was going to have to grow up before his time. That he would be forced to endure challenges that most adults never would. That he would leave the world he grew up in and knew, to live with his mom (and sometimes his dad) in a small room in a strange city for almost a year, as he fought for his life.

But, Nick had a laid-back approach that served him well. Instead of giving up or cowering in fear, he always kept a "bring it on" attitude and coped with humiliation and pain with grace and humor. A year earlier, he had spent his sixteenth birthday ravaged by chemo, too sick to leave his room at the Ronald McDonald House.

On his seventeenth birthday, he drove to school.

As I drove by the school, I saw his big old blue truck in parking space 352. I smiled, thanked God, and went about my day, knowing that life, for today, was good. My daily affirmation, "Today is a good day," was especially meaningful on that day. I thought back on seventeen years of birthdays, remembering his curly black hair, and the twinkle in his eye, and his wishes for simple gifts like roll-erblades and beach trips. As he blew out his candles for the seventeenth time, I knew his wish. It was mine too.

Our Gift

When we got home from our last antibody treatment before the holidays, my mind and heart switched into Christmas mode. It was 2006. Unlike the previous year's holiday, this Christmas was like a freeze frame back to our normal life. There was love, laughter, bickering, exhaustion, and fun. The usual elements of the season were experienced without a mention of our family being any different than others. Nick thoroughly enjoyed his winter break—stayed out late, ate Christmas cookies, and devoured holiday meals. He looked amazing.

Still, it had been hard to leave the people we had grown so close to in New York. Some of them didn't get to go home for Christmas. My joy was tempered by the ever-present knowledge that many families were not receiving the same gift that we were.

I remembered to see this remission time as our "gift." We had a window to climb through to the real world again. *Again, I reminded myself to be grateful for our life and our blessings. Even in the best of times, I knew there was nothing I could really control, except for my own reactions.*

Alexis Turns Three

After three relatively peaceful months spent mostly at home, living a mostly normal life, we had to return to New York for Nick's three-month scan and bone-marrow biopsy. That meant a return to the bottomless anxiety of not knowing, the almost unbearable tension of waiting for test results, and another trip to the "House of Pain" for the next round of antibodies.

Before we left, there was a celebration we got great joy out of hosting. My granddaughter, Alexis, was turning three. We threw her a little birthday lunch.

When she blew out the candles on her cake, we told her to make a wish. She scrunched up her face and shut her eyes extra tight. Then she said,

"Um...um...I wish for Nick to stay healthy!"

It was totally unprompted and unexpected. She was only three years old. She could have easily wished for more princess stuff, or for other toys. It was a reminder of how Nick's journey trickled down to touch even the most innocent. It was a "moment," and we all were moved.

In just a few hours Nick would morph from his happy-go-lucky self, to an achy, irritable, tired, and sullen teenager. I knew the progression. Each day his body would be assaulted. He would receive more pain medicine than most do in a lifetime. He would endure nausea, a lack of appetite, and no energy. This time, he would also endure his quarterly scans and the drilling of four holes in his hips to test his bone marrow. Each day, the hospital would feel more familiar and home would recede further and further away.

The ironic thing was that all of this took place in just five days. At the end of the week, Nick would come home, rest up, and return to school the next Monday. With his hoodie and his backpack and his truck parked in space 352, he would return to greetings from friends and plans for the weekend.

I would anxiously await the bone-marrow results.

Snow and Affirmation

We were back in the rhythm of our split screen life. Winter 2007 felt hopeful. After another week of antibodies and another set of scans with good results, we were set to head home. Since friends from home had been visiting New York, Nick and I got a ride back home—a nice change from the train. At least it was until we got closer to home and snow and ice started coming down! The last five miles down the winding roads to our house were treacherous, but we made it home just in time to watch Sunday football playoffs.

Nick and I were both exhausted, but we dealt with it in totally different ways. Whenever we got back from New York, I needed a day or so to totally isolate myself and get my head back in "home world." I'd ponder the week we had just endured and basically isolate myself.

Nick, on the other hand, just checked another round off the list and moved forward. Always, always he moved forward. After all, he had a life to live.

One of our friends came over to watch the game with us and welcome us home. He mentioned how sorry he was that Nick had to go through hell that week. He could see the bandages hanging over Nick's flannel pajama bottoms where, just two days before, bone marrow had been dug out of his hips. He was still tender and sore as he nestled onto the couch to watch the game. Still, Nick's response to our friend's comment was "That was last week!" About a half hour later, he pulled on his snowboarding pants—right over his pajamas and bandages—and went outside to do a little skating on the new snow skate he had received for Christmas.

I worried that if he fell on his tender hips he would really be hurt, but Nick didn't worry at all. He sailed down the side yard as if nothing was wrong, almost as an affirmation that he was home, living life his way.

I so wished that I could live that way. *Live in the now. Embrace the gifts of the moment. Because the moment is really all we have.*

Twenty-Seven Years and a Dream

One night, I had what I can only describe as a semiconscious dream. It was very weird. I was with some other neuroblastoma moms—we were in a dark field that was covered with land mines. There was panic because we had to get through the field. We all looked at each other, knowing we had to do it, and also knowing not all of us would make it to the other side.

I woke up not sure where I was. Then I looked over at Nick sleeping, and I realized we were back at Ronald McDonald House, still gingerly crossing the field together. It was February 2007, and we were in the ninth round of antibody treatment.

The next day was my twenty-seventh wedding anniversary, the only one Jim and I had ever spent apart. Who would have ever guessed that our "for better or for worse" would include a child with cancer, and an anniversary spent separated by hundreds of miles? Yet the experience had strengthened us as a couple and really strengthened our whole family. We learned the hard way, you simply can't sweat the small stuff, because tomorrow may knock your socks off. As for our anniversary, we would celebrate on Saturday, when Nick and I returned home. We'd pick up right where we left off a few days earlier.

I looked over at my son again. When he slept, I could still see a glimmer of the little boy in his beautiful face. I felt so proud to call him my son. It had been a hard day of antibodies, but he looked so peaceful. Every day he took the pain "like a man" and was famous for somehow finding the energy to flirt with the nurses. When he suffered, he did so in silence. When he felt better, he never looked back.

When we woke up in the morning, Nick remembered what day it was and wished me a happy anniversary. We walked up First Avenue together for the last day of his ninth round of antibody hell. After a long and painful day at the hospital, I brought Nick back to the "House" and got him to sleep with drugs, hot packs, and massage.

And then I realized—it was only six-thirty at night and it was still my anniversary.

Nick wanted the lights out and his TV shows humming in the background while he slept. I could have stayed with him in the dark and felt sorry for myself. I had a choice. I could make something happen. I picked up the book I had been reading and walked around the corner. I got a table at our neighborhood Italian restaurant, ordered a nice glass of wine, and a full course dinner and settled into my book.

I never go in restaurants to read a book and eat by myself, *never*! I know other people do, but it always felt funny to me, but honestly the experience was kind of liberating. I called Jim. He was having pizza delivery. Over the phone, I raised my lonely glass and we toasted each other laughing and making the most of our anniversary dinner. When I returned with a pepperoni pinwheel and one of my two chicken breasts for Nick, he woke up. He was able to eat and once again he wished me a happy anniversary. I kissed him goodnight and drifted off to sleep.

The next day, we would take a train around noon. We would travel south, away from this city, away from the hospital, the staff, and the treatment that made us feel secure.

How ironic! The very thing that took us away from our normal world, was the thing that made us feel secure.

Two Wheelchairs and Easter

Just before Easter, we returned for Nick's tenth round of antibodies. On the last day of the week, he had decided to give a gift to his nurse tech—an older, Jamaican woman who always referred to Nick as "my love." She was one of the angels who helped Nick cope so much during those agonizing treatments. She always knew how many hot packs to bring him, how many pillows he used (three), and how many blankets he wanted (two). She always scurried around to get our room ready for us. So, on that Friday before Easter, Nick surprised her with a cute, Easter Bunny candy dish filled with chocolate eggs. She was so touched that I thought she might cry!

Later that day when his treatment was over, he was so exhausted he decided to take a wheelchair to the hospital lobby and wait for the courtesy van to take us the five blocks back to the "House." While we waited for the van, Nick asked me to wheel him to the window of the lobby so his wheelchair would line up beside an older man's chair.

This man was all alone. He was from Cuba and had no family to drive him home. He was waiting at the window for the car service to pick him up. Nick reached out and started a conversation, and the two of them chatted for a good ten minutes. Nick told the man his "cancer story," lifting up his shirt to show his scars. The older man was very moved that someone had taken the time to talk to him. When the van arrived and Nick got up to leave, he shook the man's hand. The man looked at me with his scruffy, unshaven face and tender, tired eyes. He said, "You have a good boy there. God bless you all." It was one of those *moments* that revealed to me the person Nick had become through all of this.

I looked at the world with such a different perspective. I wanted to just shout to everyone that Easter:

Renew yourself and be thankful for the gift of a normal life! Don't dwell on the challenges, ponder the ways you can be filled to the brim with your purpose and passion. You never know when life will turn, and you will need the strength of what you have become to carry you through.

Be thankful that your world is more than just hoping to breathe another day. Expand, give, serve, and grow. Do it for those who do not have that choice, for those who must put all of their energy into sheer survival.

Crossing Over

Sundays were hard. That was the day we traded our life in Virginia for our other life in New York, departing from the familiar to the unknown.

The dread would start when I woke up on Sunday morning. I wouldn't want to get out of bed because I knew that one, single action would start the chain of events that would result in Nick and me getting on the train to New York. Almost inevitably, I would feel irritable and agitated at everything. All I wanted to do was to stomp my feet like a child and scream "I don't *want to*"!

Nick, on the other hand, was usually fine. He didn't seem to care that we would be heading back to New York in a few hours. On this particular departure day, he was helping his dad remove a log from our pond. Until that job was done, it was the only thing he cared about.

The drive to the train was, as usual, mostly silent. At one point, I noticed my jaw was clenched. When we reached the station, Jim kissed me good-bye, and I heard the familiar sound of the wheels of my suitcase rolling on the pavement. That sound—familiar and purposeful—signaled the beginning of my transition. I felt myself strengthen into "game on" mode. Once the conductor punched my ticket and the slideshow of buildings began to move outside the window, I started to calm down. Eventually, I fell into a deep sleep. When I woke up about an hour later, Nick was calmly listening to his iPod. There we were, Mom and Nick, back on our mission. We were "crossing over" again. I was no longer at home dreading the inevitable. I was coping and back on caretaker autopilot.

I always found comfort in the familiar faces in the clinic, and the collective understanding we shared. It would be a tough week with bone marrow biopsies again and another agonizing week of antibody treatment. But this was our life now. Another mother, waiting for her son's bone-marrow biopsies described the experience by saying it was just like looking at a bunch of kids waiting to get haircuts. Except these kids were routinely, nonchalantly waiting to have long needles scoop bone marrow out of their hips.

We all cross over. We have to.

IV
Relapse and Determination

The Compass Point of Family
Family is at the root of the human heart. Like the heart, some families are stronger than others. Nurturing family is what strengthens it. The heart of a family can literally be the "bypass" that helps life flow.

Waiting for scan results and biopsy results is so nerve-wracking. Your mind is hoping for one thing and one thing only: the overwhelming feeling of relief that washes over you when a scan comes back clean. You want it so much you almost expect it—especially when it's happened several times in a row. But, at the same time, you try to prepare yourself for the possibility that the news will not be good.

I found you can never really be prepared, not really.

We were in the middle of an antibody treatment when the doctor came in. He said they wanted to do another scan, as there appeared to be some uptake where it shouldn't have been. Nick looked at me and said he was scared. Later, while he slept off the day's treatment, I was taken back to the doctor's office, where I threw up and rocked back and forth. I called home, and that night Jim arrived from Virginia.

We all needed time to process and to refocus, to cross over again.

Trying to Live Like Nick

The relapse seemed to transport Nick to some deeper level of acceptance and understanding. He was the patient, but he also became our teacher, our guru, and our guide. He used the word "tranquil" while waiting for his CAT scan and insisted to everyone that he would be fine.

From this point forward, there would be new rules. Nick refused to dwell on his cancer, or even talk about it, and he expected the same from us. He wanted every minute of his life to count, so negativity was not allowed. We returned home with the news of relapse and the reality that our time in remission was over. I wanted to crumble, but not Nick. Instead, he planned to spend his last week at home before returning to New York doing the things he loved, including an all-day music festival on Saturday and a golf game on Sunday.

Coping with this latest cancer bombshell wasn't so easy for me. Before news of relapse, I had signed up to participate in my first state golf tournament in two years. The plan had been to leave early Sunday morning and not return until Tuesday evening. But after Nick's news, I couldn't even breathe normally. How could I go away with twelve women to play tournament golf for three days? The night before I was supposed to leave, I wound up in a fetal position, having a complete meltdown. While Nick was out with friends, I wailed that he was going to die. Only Jim heard me.

Then, suddenly, I thought of Nick. The last thing he would want was to see me lying around the house moping. Somehow, I mustered up the courage to "just do it." I went and I actually laughed and had moments where my mind was not thinking about everything.

Meanwhile, Nick went back to school and savored every last moment of "normal." Jeffrey came home from college, Alyson and her family gathered, and I came home in time to celebrate Jim's sixtieth birthday. He played golf with both sons in the afternoon, and Nick hit the ball really well. Life was going on.

But for me...it was hard. I really didn't know how to cope with the end of Nick's remission. I had allowed myself to be blindsided once again—I had let myself believe that we truly were in the group of patients that would stay in remission.

We all tried to Live Like Nick Did (or LLND). But I struggled. I really did.

Perspective

Life keeps going even though you may feel like you can't. Maybe that's what "living with cancer" really means. You put one foot in front of the other and cherish the moments and the hours that feel normal. You compartmentalize if you can, so you can keep moving. You recognize the smallest bits of relief and rejoice in them. Things like a good night of sleep, and watching your beloved child hurl his clubs in the back of his truck to go to the golf course take on new meaning. I would witness Nick smile and wave as he pulled out of the driveway with his music blasting and I would be reminded, there is good in today.

Then there are those less desirable aspects of normal- the unpleasant ones. Shortly after relapse, in one twenty-four-hour period, I had to contend with:

- Workers waking me up in the morning by putting new siding on the house right outside my bedroom,
- a leak that spewed water all over the kitchen floor,
- a change in our New York schedule that entailed booking new flights,
- our car tags expiring, running out of wiper fluid, and a windshield so dusty I couldn't see through it,
- the dogs running though the pond and getting mud all over everything,
- having to pay bills before leaving for New York,
- twenty-one relatives to call into the gate at the lake house for Jim's sixtieth birthday weekend, and
- squeezing in a hair appointment, since I hadn't had time to get my hair done (I wonder why!) and gray was everywhere.

A packed day like that would be hard enough to handle if everyone was healthy, but having so little energy in reserve, I spent most of the day on the edge of a meltdown.

Then Nick walked in from school whistling, barely stopping to say hello before leaving to play "disc golf." I had to pause and smile with gratitude.

Learning to Live Like Nick Did could benefit all of us.

Mother's Day 2007

When you give birth to a child, you have an instinct that kicks in. You have a primal response to love, protect, and secure that child so that he (or she) can live a life of health and happiness. What happens when that primal instinct is faced with a challenge greater than a human can imagine?

Our final week before Nick's relapse treatment began ended on Mother's Day 2007. The ten days before had us to the limits of what we could understand, process, and react to. There were moments of complete despair, paralysis of thought, and inability to act. There were moments of rational optimism, hard praying, and deep, deep fear. All of that happened inside of us. The outside world kept moving on, that part was a gift.

It was and is a gift to have plans and friends and family.

That morning, I awoke to the sounds of birds and bugs and the rooster next door. Those familiar sounds comforted me and reminded me that I was at home. When one travels between two worlds, it is sometimes the smallest of things that soothe you and tell you, "Relax, this is your real life." I cherished pouring coffee from my own pot that morning, instead of drinking out of a Styrofoam cup from the hospital, or from the corner store in the city. The feel of my favorite mug brought a smile to my face. Nick was sleeping soundly upstairs, the house was quiet…oh how I wished that was us all the time.

You have to grab the wonder and magic of the "new normal" when it is there and thank God for those moments, for they nourish you to keep going.

Later, we went to the lake to celebrate Mother's Day. Nick played golf, went tubing on the lake, played Frisbee on the beach, laughed with his niece and nephew, and chilled out with all of us, always with a smile on his face. I took it all in through a mother's eyes—eyes that filled with tears more than once, but were still able to clearly see.

We *had* to keep living life.

That weekend validated my belief that life really is a series of moments, strung together. It wasn't about next year, next month, next week, or even tomorrow. It was about now. We knew we were facing hard times. We knew getting Nick back to remission would be a tough fight. We had to research and explore all options, and I knew that would take up most of my mental energy and time.

At that moment, on that Mother's Day, God whispered to me to not waste the time when Nick was feeling so normal. I was able to sit back and absorb the special experiences that weekend brought to us. Each of those many minutes turned into hours, which turned into two beautiful days together.

It was a very happy Mother's Day.

Living a Double Life

Relapse or no relapse, life went on. Memorial Day, typically a day of remembrance and of the anticipation of summer- felt very different this year. While I struggled with the fear of the unknown, wondering how we all managed to keep going, Nick went to the lake with friends and his brother. They were gone for two days. It was so comforting to think of him down there without parents, without nagging, without reminders of the disease inside of him. At home Jim and I kept busy, playing golf, visiting with family, and resting. A stranger looking in would see a typical family, on a typical holiday weekend. That image would not reflect the constant terror inside of us. We had learned to push it down, to put it away for brief moments.

Then something would happen, and we'd have that burning panic all over again.

That weekend, that "something" was the news that a truly beautiful family lost their daughter to the same hideous disease that was ravaging our son. I got the news just as we were heading to my cousin's house for a picnic. I was devastated; it was horrible news, but I didn't want to bring the world down with me. So, I watched Nick kicking the soccer ball with Alexis and chilling with his family. I smiled and laughed and made sure I looked fine. But deep down, my heart was filled with despair and sadness and wondering. Was Nick's relapse slow growing? What shape was it taking inside my precious child's body? Would he be blessed with stable or NED status for a long time? What did the next few months look like?

Then I pulled my thoughts back to that day, that event, that time together. I moved, I breathed, and I found gratitude in the day.

The next day, Nick was back at school. No one could tell he was sick again—at that point he had no symptoms. I tried to be thankful for that. There were moments when leading my double life was almost more than I could manage. Then, I would look at my son and be reassured, today we are on the side that is good.

Thank you, God.

Me Time

With all the insanity swirling around me, time alone was something I never seemed to find. I usually chose to stay very busy. But one day, I found myself in the colorful island hammock that's strung up on our back porch, overlooking our pond. I read and drifted off with a breeze blowing...it was so peaceful. I found myself praying out loud. No one was around to disturb that welcome flow of energy with spirit.

The late spring of 2007 was a transformational time for us all, but especially me. I saw Nick looking and acting so healthy, yet I knew a battle was raging inside of him. That made it especially difficult to get my mind and my spirit aligned in a positive direction.

Then, I remembered Nick's tattoo.

Friends. Family. Courage. Strength. Faith. Those were the compass points that kept us all grounded so that we could find the horizon, even during turbulent times.

I rallied and took my grandchildren to the fair that had come to our town. I rode the rides with my three-year-old granddaughter for the first time, sheer joy...a memory made.

Two Rounds of Low-Dose Chemo, One Fabulous Make-A-Wish Trip to Jamaica!

Our family rocking our tattoos in Jamaica

The relapse protocol was a lower dose of chemo to chip away at the small amount of disease. We returned for two rounds in New York, but also began the process of working with a team at Georgetown, an hour away from our home in Virginia. In the midst of the logistics of this new protocol, we also were working on the logistics of an incredible gift—a Make-A-Wish-Trip! Nick recovered easily from the first two rounds, and we were given the green light to enjoy a welcome time away! While he didn't hand out toys on the inpatient floor like he had imagined, he was allowed to invite two friends to go with him to Jamaica, and that was truly a gift to them and for all of us!

Make-A-Wish made it happen, allowing family and friends to gather together in Jamaica. We arrived to the gentle breezes and generous hearts of the island. We were so grateful for this generous gift. It was a beautiful dream come true, that included a fully staffed villa on the water, and a week without mentioning anything medical.

We were able to disconnect from pain and fear and unknown outcomes and reconnect to joy, laughter, and sheer relaxation. You don't realize just how tired your body is until you stop, relax, and feel the difference.

We were there…laughing and resting.

We were there…forgetting that we were any different.

We were there…creating memories to carry us through.

We were there…being nourished by sun, salt, heat, excellent food, and excellent rum punch!

We were there…taking in the breathtaking views of the ocean splashing against the shore as we teed up the golf ball on picture postcard-worthy holes.

We were there…being cooked for, laundered for, straightened up for, cleaned up for.

We were there…our family, happy as one.

One week later we were back home. The first round of chemo administered at Georgetown greeted us, jolting us back to reality. I felt ill just walking into a sterile environment again, our sun-drenched bodies still glowing. But this was our new world, our new routine, and we needed to accept it. It was time to get back to work.

Back to the Battle

Our wonderful doctor at Georgetown, Dr. Corina Gonzales, suggested that we use a home health nurse and get the lower dose chemo at home. This would give Nick more free time, not shuttling back and forth two hours a day. We got that approval and the first week of treatment from home began. There were no more hours of interstate travel, no more sterile hospital halls. So why was I still just as bone tired?

My system must have been in shock. One week before I was on "Fantasy Island," loving the pampered life in Jamaica; the next week I was back on caretaker duty. Nick was proactive and handled as much on his own as he could. I went right back into the motherly mode of encouraging fluids, making sure he ate, helping when he threw up, and straightening up the constant medical clutter.

That first week back was also tough for Nick. Although the treatment was much less harsh, he still had side effects. In those few days, he went from tanned and smiling to begging for nausea meds and the need to sleep. On Friday, after his drip ended, he felt well enough to start texting friends and made plans to go out. He threw up several times while he was trying to nap. Then, like he always did, he got up, changed his clothes, and headed out to join his buddies. I was so happy, I told him to just go and be a teenager. But a few minutes later, he was back home asking what he could take for nausea. He fell asleep again, then woke up, asked for dinner, ate, and headed back out with his friends.

Jim and I just sat there, amazed and exhausted.

Hospital Stays and Camp Visits

As it turned out Nick had been feeling lousy for a reason. Shortly after the post-Jamaica round of chemo, he was rushed to the hospital in septic shock. He had low blood counts and an intestinal infection. It was scary and debilitating.

A week later, Nick walked out of the hospital on his own. The doctors and nurses had worked very hard to get him out of septic shock, and they tested for any and all possible causes. They still were not exactly sure what caused it, but for us, we were ready to turn the page and focus on the good.

Part of the good, for Nick, came in the form of a visit to Camp Varsity. He got to spend time with his "camp people" and have lunch there. The staff and campers had prepared a care package for him with an amazing scrapbook of letters of hope and other well wishes, along with photos and other "artifacts" of the camp. It was the best medicine possible. He made plans to return to camp after our trip to New York for post-relapse scans. Those scans terrified me, but for Nick, whatever the news was, the show would go on.

Good News, Hidden in a Big Pile of Horrible

It felt surreal being back in New York, sleeping at the Ronald McDonald House yet again. As we adjusted our minds and prepared for the post-relapse scans, Nick awoke in the middle of the night with the symptoms of a bowel obstruction or infection. This was a major medical emergency and required a massive surgery. Thirty-five centimeters of his intestines had to be removed. That led to twelve days of sadness, pain, and utter disappointment as Nick missed the rest of the summer at camp.

Still, there was some good news—Nick's scans (the reason we went back to New York in the first place) were greatly improved. This was the exact outcome we had been hoping for...just wrapped in a big pile of horrible.

So many times I asked myself why all of this kept happening to Nick. Staying upbeat and laid back were his weapons of choice, but after battling for two years he was starting to wear down. During his hospital stay for the bowel obstruction, there were times when he was agitated, somber, lonely, and uncertain of how everything would play out when school started again. He was almost bald, down to 117 pounds, and extremely weak. Still, overall, he was calm more than agitated, happy (relatively speaking) more than somber, and starting to believe he would get home and have a sliver of summer left.

Sometimes, the hardest part was the fact that he was just a teenager. He had lost control of his independence just at the moment most kids are striving their hardest to achieve it. Sometimes, what seemed perfectly logical to me seemed anything but logical to Nick. For example:

- If he were an adult, the idea of consulting with a nutritionist to help keep his weight up would be logical.
- The suggestion of acupuncture to help keep his bowels healthy would be logical.
- The suggestion of adding high-calorie nutritional "shakes" to his diet would be logical.

However, Nick was just a few months shy of turning eighteen, and he perceived these carefully considered and very logical suggestions as an unwelcome infringement on his independence. I continued to nag, and he continued to rebel.

Which was all completely normal, in a twisted sort of way.

A Meeting That Changed Everything

The summer of Nick's relapse, I entered a new territory of Cancer World—the land of gritty, panicked, but determined "relapse parents." We all were desperate to do something more than sit and watch the life slowly leave our children. We just didn't know what to do.

One night, Dr. Cheung, the researcher who had created the antibody that Nick had received, came to speak at the Ronald McDonald House. Somehow, in my fog, I was able to secure the conference room and spread the word to parents. The room was packed with parents who sat anxiously, notebooks in hand. We had one big question for the doctor. What would it take to bring the next phase of his antibody treatment to our children? He calmly answered with a single word: "money." We asked how much it would take. After some discussion, it was determined that it would take three to five million dollars to fund his humanized antibody treatment. This treatment held more promise than the antibody trial that was the current protocol. It would serve not only children in their initial treatment, but also for children, like Nick, who had relapsed.

From that moment on, the "House" was buzzing. Kitchen chatter, clinic chatter, focused on what could be done to make it happen. Parents with vacant stares and little hope were suddenly talking about next steps and what they might do to help. From this new-found hope and energy, an idea was formed. A group of dads, mostly with children who had relapsed, decided to raise awareness for our cause by riding their bikes across the entire United States! They called their journey "The Loneliest Road." Online campaigns were launched to raise money, and the ride was set for September.

The summer of 2007 began with renewed energy and hope, as Nick battled on.

Small Victories

After a month of some of the cruelest days Nick had to endure thus far, we were finally back home. The trip was a blur—it had been such a challenge getting Nick up, hailing a cab across the city and preboarding the train. He was coping with surgical pain and coming down off of all the drugs from the hospital, while navigating New York City crowds in the heat of summer. It was a test of our patience and strength, but we made it onto the train, and once we were heading south I could finally breathe a sigh of relief.

How odd is that—a sigh of relief? What the hell does that really mean? In a cancer family, there are so many sighs of relief for all the small victories that give you hope to get through another day. You craft life around a series of small, defined accomplishments—getting through a round of treatment, getting out of the hospital, having a three-week break, getting through another scan. *You try to never let yourself go to that place where you look at "the big picture"—because the possibilities are too, too horrible. You live within, and are grateful for, those small victories, battle by battle.*

We had been battling this way for two straight years. Nick had not known a normal teenage life for more than a two to three week span since he was fifteen. This latest experience, a bowel obstruction as a result of the radiation he received at his tumor site, seemed especially cruel and unfair. Over the course of our two-year battle, I had discovered that often the treatments we relied on to save our loved ones from cancer could be as deadly as the disease. Other parents agreed—we needed less toxic options. There had to be a better way to save our children. That reality became our battle cry. Exhausted and terrified parents spread the word about the Loneliest Road campaign and encouraged everyone to donate to the first effort that would help fund the humanized antibody.

It felt daunting, but that didn't stop us.

Through it all, Nick never quit. Two years in and he was still in the game, still in the battle. Back at home, he continued to heal from the unexpected, traumatic surgery. He tried to eat more and gain weight and some muscle back. One day he announced he was going to walk the half mile to the end of our road and then back. This used to be his normal walk to the bus stop. Now it was a challenge, and a goal he set for himself. When he returned, he had an affirmative smile on his face, validating that he was gaining some control of his life once again. We continued to celebrate his small victories, and the calm and peace they brought to our day.

Waiting

When you find out your child has cancer, you put your life, your dreams, and your future on hold. You wait to resume relationships with friends and family and to experience the rituals of life BC (before cancer). It feels like you are always waiting to return to the life you "had."

At some point, you realize that the life you had is gone forever.

There is no going back. Friendships change—some for the better, some just disappear. Coping with cancer means you are too occupied, distracted, and exhausted to work at the things in life that require emotional effort—especially the ones not required for your survival.

That summer, battling to get Nick back to remission was completely exhausting. The hardest part was the waiting. Waiting for him to gain weight. Waiting for test results. Waiting for his second remission.

Waiting to plan to live like we used to.

At the same time, there were moments when we fully embraced our life, as it was. When we summoned enough emotional reserve to actually embrace life *with* cancer, we felt like a normal family. We spent a weekend at the lake, even though Nick couldn't get in the water because of his low white blood count and surgery scar. Before cancer, we may have felt that was a reason to stay home, but not this time. We didn't wait. We went, and Nick got to enjoy the change of scenery and the fellowship of family.

People often said, "I don't know how you do it." Seeing us out and about and functioning in the normal world sometimes confused people. Honestly, we were not especially resilient or superhuman. We just got tired of waiting. Nick didn't wait, why should we?

Was it hard? Yes. Did we ever have to put on a happy face when we really wanted to be in bed napping? Yes. Did we have to pump each other up and work on keeping our chins up? Yes! But for us, there wasn't really much of a choice. The alternative was to sit around and wait for things that may or may not happen.

I was (and am) so blessed to have my family. Everyone pulled together, which created the engine that drove our functional existence. We pulled each other up and created good times together. Our anxiety lessened when we were together, and we felt less helpless and paralyzed. Although we experienced an unimaginable pain, after that horrific summer of medical complications, we managed to get back up and stop "waiting" for things to get better.

Leading the charge, as always, was Nick. We watched his example, as he joined the high-school golf team, showing up at practice before he could even swing a club. He was happy just to be a part of something. He didn't wait to have hair and twenty more pounds on his six-foot frame. As hard as it was to show up for his junior year of high-school bald and twenty pounds lighter, he did it anyway. *He didn't wait to have a different life because this was his life.* There was no old life "before cancer."

For Nick, there was only the life he now had.

Caryn Franca

Back to School—Again

Late summer light was still shining in his window. Nick went to bed early, anticipating the first day of his junior year. I was in his room, preparing his morning medications, when he said the most poignant thing to me. He was getting his backpack ready. He sighed and said, "I wish I didn't feel so awful, so I could at least be a little bit excited about school."

I flashed back to Nick as a little boy, getting so excited about the first day of school. Now it took everything he had just to get to bed without throwing up again. I asked him if he wanted to stay home and sleep in. Without a word, he shook his head no. I kissed his forehead, told him how much I loved him, and walked out of his room, finally releasing the tears I had managed to hold back until then.

The next morning I woke him up. I asked him again if he wanted to stay home. Again, he said no. He was leaving early to pick up a friend and go to the 7-Eleven before school. He downed all of his pills, made another bathroom visit, tightened the belt on his jeans so they wouldn't fall off, and walked out of the house. His blue truck drove off, leaving me full of thoughts that refused to stay suppressed and tears that snuck down my cheeks without warning.

By that Friday, Nick was so weak and sick that he had to come home from school early. He simply had pushed too hard. Later that afternoon, I was out picking up some of his medications, and I passed by his high school. Everyone was walking from their neighborhoods to the year's first football game. I watched kids and teens goofing around, seeming to have not a care in the world. My emotions were raw, and I felt angry, reflective, and just sad. Their biggest concern was where to meet up with friends, while Nick's concerns were more about how to make it two more hours, before collapsing from exhaustion.

When I got home, I told Nick how sad I was that he was missing the game. I said I was sorry, I knew he must have felt isolated, almost like, in that moment, he had no friends. Nick rolled his eyes (as he often did at me) and said, "Look at my cell phone." He then proceeded to scroll through dozens and dozens of names.

He told me not to worry. He had friends.

God, I so loved that boy. Most normal teenagers would stay home if they had the slightest belly ache. Most normal teenagers would be embarrassed to walk into school on the first day with a bald head and a six-foot frame carrying 120 pounds. Most normal teenagers would never know what it took for Nick to just show up and get through his day.

I reminded myself that Nick attracted good, Nick attracted miracles, and Nick didn't allow anything to consume him. He lived for the day, sometimes, the hour, sometimes the minute.

That took immense courage.

The Loneliest Road and the Band of Parents

Dr. Kusher getting a ride on the four-wheeler

Friends and family at the finish line

The same week that Nick started his junior year of high school, the five "Loneliest Road" dads took off on their bike ride across the country. On September 10, 2007, the journey began. The money, the energy, and the publicity soared. The ride was set to end in Washington, DC. Dr. Kushner planned to come down from New York and ride the last few miles with the dads. Since this was all happening in our neck of the woods, I volunteered to hold a celebration party on our property. I will never forget that day. Dr. Kushner bounced in the Moon Bounce I rented, and Nick gave Dr. Kushner and several children rides around our property on his four-wheeler. There were pony rides and there was face painting and there were families bonding. Our community of warriors was strengthened by this accomplishment. Tears, sweat, and determination launched a movement. The Loneliest Road was a success. A heightened sense of awareness now spread nationwide. From this amazing event, Band of Parents was officially born.

We named our fund-raising organization Band of Parents because we had been inspired by the movie *Band of Brothers*. From the group's inception, we knew this much: We were not only fighting to save our own children, but the children who had yet to be diagnosed. Our organization had a very large job to do. It wasn't always easy. We were all stressed, worried, and exhausted from the strain of our children's treatment. But, we learned that sometimes, in the midst of battle, you can do superhuman things.

Like the soldiers in that movie, the whole cancer experience was a lot like we imagined war to be. We had all been strangers just months, weeks, even hours before. We came to know each other under the most intimate and dire of circumstances. We lived in close quarters, separated by curtains in the hospital, and by thin walls at the Ronald McDonald House. We all had been given the same "battle plan." We were bound together by fear, but also hope. We all had a common understanding of the enemy. Together, we marched through the war that is cancer. We leaned on each other, we cried with each other, and we communicated the message "I know how you feel right now" with just a glance.

I remember the first time we lost one of our own on the battlefield. We tried to help, to be there for the parents, but there was nothing that could be done, not really. Each time we lost one of our own, we each shared the paralyzing knowledge that someone could be there with us one day and gone the next. We each knew our child could be next. We were down, but our only choice was to get back up and keep fighting.

I struggled to frame my life with gratitude, even though sadness overshadowed every single part of my being sometimes. *I searched for the smallest of things to be grateful for each day. Even on the very best of days, there was a dark undercurrent always rumbling. Gratitude helped to quiet the rumble, snuff out the sadness, and helped me go about living my life, mostly like everyone else did.*

At the same time, there was a sense of urgency surrounding the work I was doing, together with new comrades. Our commitment to help drive the antibody project to fruition was not something we took lightly. I felt empowered, knowing I was a part of a group that could truly make a difference in how neuroblastoma would be treated in the future. Through treatment and tragedy, our "Band of Parents" would persevere. We were only a small group of parents, yet we planted seeds of great hope and change.

A Muffler, a Deer, and a Goal

Sometimes, focusing on a small goal can help you get through your darkest times. For Nick, that goal came in the form of a muffler. For about a year, he'd been hanging on to a souped-up, slightly illegal muffler, waiting to install it on his truck (it needed to be welded). But it still hadn't happened.

Every month, when he had his chemo infusion treatment, he would come up with a list of "Things to Accomplish" around his treatment to keep him focused and looking ahead. That month, he decided his accomplishment would be to finally get that muffler installed.

I thought it would be rough during chemo for him to follow me in his truck, drop it off, and pick it up later, all while taking a multitude of drugs to keep his nausea away. But Nick insisted he could handle it. He made the appointment and we dropped his truck off on the way to the infusion clinic.

During his chemo infusion, he kept saying, "Uh, I feel so sick." I told him not to worry about the truck. I told him to rest and let me get him home, we would pick up the truck over the weekend. But he asked me to call the mechanic to see if his truck was ready, and it was. When the pump beeped, and the chemo drip ended, Nick emerged from the nest of blankets he had made. He looked at me and said, "Let's do it."

The look on his face when he got in his truck, pressed the gas, and heard the sound of his new muffler was one I will never forget. Just an hour before he was miserable and sick, snuggled under a blanket and breathing deeply to keep himself from throwing up. Now he gave me a full-blown Nick smile, one I hadn't seen since the Monday before, when he started the round of chemo.

That was how Nick rolled. *He set goals; benchmarks of normalcy helped steer him through his journey.*

By Saturday, he was feeling much better. He got up that morning, showered, and with a very loud muffler, drove his blue truck to visit some buddies at the University of Virginia (UVA). Later, he called to tell me that he had arrived safely and also mentioned, in a very matter-of-fact way, that on the way there, he hit a deer going sixty miles an hour. He told me his air bag did not deploy, but the deer had flown at least one hundred feet behind the truck and died. Nick pulled over to gather himself and then continued on to UVA.

That was Nick...deal with what you have to, and then keep driving toward your goal.

Massive Cookie Baking

Meanwhile, Band of Parents continued marching forward. An online merchandise shop was launched, and soon, nearly every parent at the hospital was wearing some form of our logo on a hat, a sweatshirt or a T-shirt. That we were finally doing something productive was empowering when hope was thin. But there were constant reminders of the seriousness of the battle we were fighting. One "Loneliest Road " dad experienced the tragic loss of their sweet daughter, shortly after he returned from the cross-country ride. Two others took turns for the worse. It was clear that time was critical, and we needed to get the money raised, as fast as we could.

A family with ties to the cooking industry helped us launch an online-ordering site for holiday cookies. The response was amazing, and by December 2007, Band of Parents had raised close to $400,000. That initial cookie sale eventually grew into an amazing organization all its own. Sadly, that family's child also passed before the antibody was funded, but their work continued and still continues today.

Nick at Eighteen

Nick came into our lives five and a half years after we thought we were finished having children. Since he was a Christmas baby, we named him Nicholas, and from the beginning, he was a go-with-the-flow kind of child. That quality stuck with him through childhood and was there, battered but unbowed, as we celebrated his eighteenth birthday.

That year, as I decorated our Christmas tree, unwrapping the "Baby's First

Christmas 1989" ornament, and the "Soccer Star" ornament, and all the crafty little classroom-made ornaments I had saved through the years. I was filled with nostalgia. I remembered when life was peaceful and simple. When all was calm, all was bright, just like the carol says.

As a parent, you weave together a tapestry of experiences that become the foundation for your child's values in life. Nick's childhood was filled with family, faith, fun, and friendship. It is no surprise that those values served as his foundation as he navigated the uncertain path he was forced to travel. He carried them across his back on his tattoo, and he carried them in life as an example to all of us.

On his eighteenth birthday, calm and bright were no longer words I would use to describe our family, but there were other victories. Nick was there to put ornaments on the tree. He was there to blow out candles. He was there to shake packages and share another birthday and another Christmas. Friends, family, faith...he continued to weave his tapestry without anger and without questioning.

On December 4, 2007, our Christmas miracle legally became a man. The depth of love we felt on that day is still so hard to describe. He was now taking just an oral chemo that was keeping his very minimal disease stable, and he felt strong and healthy most of the time. *We couldn't look forward, and it was painful to look back at the way things had been and the promise life once held. We could only focus on the gift that each new day with Nick brought to us.*

A Cherry-Red Malibu amid the Battle

drag racing car

Nick had a passion for auto mechanics. He received an award in auto mechanics in school and dreamed of feeling the exhilaration of drag racing. As an eighteenth birthday surprise, Jim arranged for that dream to come true. He was able to purchase a 1994 cherry-red Malibu and have it delivered to our house in front of family and friends. His look of surprise and childlike excitement gave us all a moment of untainted happiness. For that moment, there was no beast lurking, only a pure and overpowering sense of joy. The car represented freedom and adventure. Plans were made to take it to the local track and learn the art of drag racing. He now had a new goal, and a new way to live fearlessly, amid his battle. Word had spread about his first weekend race. Friends and family gathered at the track. I was worried about his lower than normal platelet count: would he crash, would he bruise and bleed? I was worried about his ability to focus with other cars racing beside him. I was…the mom. As the flag dropped and the front end of his car literally lifted, I held my breath. The smoke, noise, and speed seemed to last forever. In reality it was a just a few seconds. The start and finish is quick. He did well, and emerged from the car more of a man. I looked at him getting out of the car. Everyone was hugging and high-fiving him as I approached.

I hugged him hard and was relieved and so very proud to witness his coming of age in that car. There would be more races, and more worry on my part. It was a constant struggle to live as spontaneous and as courageous as my son. I was. . .the mom.

Life sometimes surprises you with unimagined joy, amid the battle.

New Boots for a New Year

Christmas 2007 had been full of love, friendship, and magic. Our house was filled with family, visitors, and many meals were shared. But, my favorite memory of that Christmas is a shopping trip with Nick. One of his goals was to finally go snowboarding again that winter. His boots had been sitting in his closet, untouched, and were now too small. So, I took him to pick out new snowboarding boots a few days before Christmas. Nick naturally struck up a conversation with the "dude" at the snowboard shop, and they swapped stories of mountains they shredded and shared their plans for the winter. Sitting on the bench listening, I realized that, to the shop dude, Nick was another eighteen-year-old who had outgrown his boots. The young man had no idea of Nick's other life. In fact, Nick even asked for an application to work there. That was a magical moment for me—seeing how poised, self-assured, and natural he was.

That was one of the memories I held on to, knowing that we would return to treatment right after the new year. I thanked God for a holiday that provided us all with a frozen frame of normalcy. Nick had mastered the art of living in between treatments. I needed to learn to follow his lead.

I started 2008 with a list of affirmations of how I wanted to go forth and show up in the world. They were:

- Be humble, be generous, be kind, and appreciative of the days that are given to you when nothing is bad.
- Think twice before complaining about boredom.
- Open your heart to others.
- Fight for others who can't fight by themselves.

Those thoughts were on my mind on the first day of that new year.

Put on Those New Boots and Glide

Since setting short-term goals and focusing on things that could be controlled seemed to be working well for Nick, I redoubled my own efforts to function in the same way. That feeling of freedom Nick got from snowboarding was motivation to create a winter get-away with the family. Nick's most recent scans had come back stable, and that meant he could continue with his oral chemo and continue living his version of a normal life. We all went to the mountains, and instead of bunking with us, Nick shared a condo with the other young people, which gave him freedom and a sense of being "one of the guys." Their condo looked like a fraternity house by the last day, but I tried hard not to worry about germs, and his weakened immune system, which was a constant concern at that point because of the oral chemo. If I had any doubts that Nick was okay, they were quickly put to rest when, while slowly making my S turns across the mountain, I heard a whoosh go by—and it was Nick. He was on his snowboard, hugging the edge of the mountain, going straight down at high speed. *I just stopped and watched him, tall and thin, gliding effortlessly down the slope. He faced life that same way. He looked fear in the eye and defied it. He found the thrills, the fun, the people who made his life worth living and embraced them each day.*

Not a word was spoken about cancer for five days. No one he met had a clue. He was just an eighteen-year-old cutie, hanging out in the lodge like all the others. It was a wonderful time of gratitude, and freedom for all of us.

How Do We Do It?

When we spent time with friends and relatives, between the fun times and the laughter and the food, eventually, the conversation would get more serious, and often would involve a question I still can't even answer:

"How do you do it?"

How did we cope, function, and go about semi-normal routines in life? One of the first skills we needed to master was the ability to absorb unthinkable news and keep going. How many times had we been knocked down in that way? And yet, there we were, still moving forward. Nick was back at school, I was working on a training and a local concert fundraiser for Band of Parents. If a person had taken a peek into our life, it would have looked normal.

What people didn't see is that we had learned to function and grieve simultaneously. *We adjusted to new surroundings and created a world of survival wherever we were lead, because honestly, that's human nature.* Each time we received the dreaded, horrible news that one of our own had been taken by this disease, we grieved, but we kept moving forward. It was survival, and it was what we learned we had to do. How did we do it? We grabbed every single molecule of good out of each person and each experience to sustain us, as we waded through the horrors and watched our friends fall.

And always, we wondered...*who will be next?*

Spreading His Wings

In March, Nick announced he was going to visit friends at UVA for the weekend. He came home from school, power napped, and then packed up to go. Later, he came into my office, backpack slung over his broad shoulders, and gave me a kiss and a smile. When he turned to leave, he looked like any other eighteen-year-old, except for the blue seven-day pill pack of chemo meds tucked into the mesh side compartment of his backpack.

He was eighteen. He wanted to be independent. As he drove away, I knew I just had to trust. I trusted he would remember to take all his pills. I trusted that he would use good judgment with "college behavior" and I trusted that he would embrace every moment. He had so much wisdom, so much maturity—he had more than earned his freedom.

When he returned, Jim and I left for a week-long trip south to watch Nick's cousin graduate from Marine boot camp, and relax and play golf. It felt weird after so much intense time together to drive away from him. But, we were determined to embrace living like Nick did. While we were away, Nick got himself up, figured out how to feed himself, got his homework done, and even took care of his dogs and his cat. He was fine, he had crossed over, he was a man, and he was responsible. *He never asked for the life he got, but he had learned to roll with most anything.*

Spring, 2008

After a nice run of normal, things got harder again. His stable disease erupted into progression, and suddenly, Nick was back in more aggressive chemo, dealing with low blood counts, including one so low it resulted in another hospital stay. He was also tackling college prep class and preparing for end of school exams. We all were exhausted, with our hope and faith fading away. One evening, when we gathered to say our blessing before dinner, Nick just said, "Why bother? Prayer doesn't do anything."

But then, as it had so often done, Nick's compass turned again. He returned from the hospital surrounded by friends and family. He played golf, studied, prepared for the SAT, and even started gaining weight again.

Predictions often do not match outcomes. I remember a day that spring when the forecast was for severe thunderstorms and torrential downpours. Instead, I looked out my office window at an awesome full moon and clear skies. It never rained.

So why sit and wait for the lightning and thunder? If you keep marching forward, sometimes the rain never comes. Sometimes you build new experiences and new memories, just by ignoring the warnings and enjoying the moments as they happen.

Find parts of life that are good. Don't sit and wait for the storm to arrive. Play on, rain or shine.

Rocks in Puddles

One day that spring, while taking a walk with my grandchildren, we discovered a mud puddle. We stopped to play, and for over a half an hour, I marveled at their complete joy—just throwing rocks in a mud puddle. It made me ponder and reflect. Small children have a way of squeezing fun out of the tiny experiences. They transform themselves into imaginary characters, delight in whatever happens to be in their environment, and focus completely on the joy of the here and now. As they laughed and splashed and forgot everything else, I was reminded of the sheer power of living in the moment, like a child.

Nick was so good at living like that, in the here and now. He'd grab his fishing pole, he'd go hit balls, he'd tinker with his truck. He stayed in motion, enjoying small things, focusing on what brought positive feelings to his life, a life he navigated well. He found the joy, even amid the dark times.

Throw some rocks in a puddle, watch the sun set, snuggle a little closer. Find joy in the moments.

Not Your Normal Senior

The joy of camp and the reality of senior year

By the summer of 2008, Nick was stable again, getting low-dose chemo every three weeks to try and keep him that way. That meant he was finally able to live his dream and serve as a counselor at Camp Varsity for five whole weeks. Every week he had to leave camp and drive himself to the hospital for blood count checks. Once again that summer, he decided to keep his cancer a secret. When the little boys in the cabin he supervised asked about his very large scar, he employed his favorite explanation—he had been bitten by a shark. That way he was able to be normal at camp, which was incredibly healing.

He came home after five weeks with his other "family" in the Blue Ridge Mountains. That was the longest I had ever been separated from him. His hair had grown back, he had gained weight, and he even had a slight beard.

Nick was less than enthusiastic about heading back to high school for his senior year. For Jim and I, it was a joy and a miracle to reach this milestone, but for Nick…not so much. Because he missed an entire year of school during his first year of treatment, he still had one more year of high school to complete. His friends and classmates were going off to college. Just a few months shy of his nineteenth birthday, he still had to chip away at that last year of high school, and he wasn't thrilled. But Nick was Nick, and I knew he would handle it.

Meanwhile, I celebrated inside. I had waited for the day my son would start his senior year. In our darker times, we questioned whether it would ever come. When it did, my house was quiet and I was happy.

Nick spent the last few days of summer two hours away, visiting James Madison University, staying with some of his buddies who were freshmen there. He also played on his high-school golf team and met with his SAT tutor. Senior year had arrived, and my desperate plea was for everything to stay "normal."

Not so normal was the fact that Nick was also facing his thirteenth round of post relapse chemo just two weeks into his senior year. Not so normal was the fact that, at the end of September, we would return to New York to have every cell of his body evaluated. *Dancing in the normal world, with not so normal circumstances was indeed, our "normal." Accepting this reality helped us find meaning and joy in the twisted normal world that was us.*

Those dates on the calendar where chemo and scans were penciled in were almost the only reminder that Nick was not a normal high-school senior. Beyond that, it was easy to be fooled. He seemed so much like everyone else that it was easy to go into a place of denial where I was free from the burden I carried. I still felt the terror and the butterflies welling in my gut whenever I let myself "go there." But going into denial wasn't any safer. Scans were approaching, and I knew we all had to come out from our blanket of security to face whatever came next. We would rejoice for the good news we expected. We would look at a new treatment plan for the fall. We would forge forward, balancing our two worlds.

And until that time, he would remain a normal, albeit a little older than most, senior in high school. And I was grateful.

Back in the Big Apple

At this point, most of our treatment was done at Georgetown, our home hospital. I was so grateful to have the most kind and wonderful oncologist guiding us there. However, we still were going to New York for most scans. So, on September 30, four weeks into Nick's senior year, we left once again for the Big Apple.

The population at the Ronald McDonald House had changed, but the faces—with that common look of vacant shock—were the same. How do you go from living a normal life, raising your "healthy" child to living in New York, in a house that by definition, means you have a very sick child?

Nick and I had also changed. Since we now had most of our treatment at home, we were not as familiar with the faces, but the five-block walk, and the determined way we set our jaw was no different than it had been four years before. Friends still surrounded us, including dear ones in Westchester, who we joined for dinner while there. Nick even had a friend from home going to college in New York, and he visited and hung out. Those few hours of friendship, conversation, and support kept us going as we awaited the results of yet another set of scans—scans we hoped would he the ticket to another three months of freedom.

Ultimately, those scans gave conflicting results. We consulted with our New York and Georgetown radiologists, and after much discussion, it was decided that we would keep Nick on low-dose, oral chemo and await a new clinical trial starting in Philadelphia the following spring.

Reflections on Our Fourth Christmas in Treatment

Gratitude:

We have learned to be thankful for moments, days and weeks where life appears normal. We have learned to be so grateful for the weeks where scans aren't looming, where there is positive news from our other friends battling, where we rest at night sometimes without fear. We have discovered friends in hidden places. We have seen old friends remain steadfast. We have family that has their priorities straight and hearts that sing, and hearts that cry, in tempo with every new twist and turn on our road. For all of this and more we are grateful.

Generosity:

The generous efforts of so many, near and far lighten our load. The gestures of support through notes, meals, and fundraising have touched us and changed us. Generosity has a new meaning for us. It means stepping into another's world to offer guidance along this path. It means taking extra time to let others know how much we appreciate them. Generosity is one of the threads that holds us together and one we have learned to participate in, in more rich and meaningful ways.

Grace:

Understanding the need for grace in life has become so clear through this journey. A quiet moment of silent understanding with another family, a look of compassion between two sets of eyes in pain, forgiveness to others who don't know how to be who we need them to be. These are moments where grace rings loudly and we have peace, where before we would have had anger, sorrow, fear. Grace also has taught us to rest in what is good, find peace amid the chaos that is our life, touch others with the spirit in which we wish to be touched… with kindness, compassion and quiet understanding.

V
New Beginnings

The Compass Point of Strength

Sometimes you literally feel your emotional muscles flexing, trying to find the strength to carry on. To witness suffering causes many to run. Find that inner strength, don't let circumstances thwart a gift you can give. Hold others up, until they have the strength to do so again. Strength is summoned sometimes in the darkest of times. Don't be afraid to lean in, so someone can lean, on you, until their own strength emerges again.

January 2009

The year 2008 had been good, with more and more milestones piling up. Nick voted in his first presidential election. He was accepted to Lynchburg College. We all finished out the year on a high note. But just when we were breathing a little easier, our first trip back to New York in 2009 brought devastating news. Nick's disease had broken through the oral chemo. He needed a round of medium-dose chemotherapy, which meant another trip to New York, where we always felt most comfortable having more intense therapies administered. I felt like I'd been punched in the gut. My head was once again filled with what-ifs. I felt myself tumbling back into darkness and exhaustion.

Nick simply stated, "We'll do what we have to do."

Climbing Out of Darkness

Looking back through my journal, I discovered that I didn't write a lot about the days when I just couldn't pull it together. There were a lot of them when Nick was sick. There were days when I couldn't find a reason to get dressed, or get off the couch. Some days I could not focus on anything but the news that brought such devastation to my life once again. I couldn't eat, I didn't smile, I just watched the day tick by, numb.

At some point, earlier in this journey, I learned that I had to give myself permission to fall apart for a day or so. But, after that day or two, I knew I had to pull it together. Sadly, there was no guide explaining how to cope with the sucker-punch, knock-the-breath-out-of-you news, transitioning back to relapse and away from the temporary calm that we all had enjoyed.

This time, the transition started simply, with a cup of tea and a talk with my husband, who gently reminded me that our main purpose was to be who Nick needed us to be. It continued through a carry-out dinner (since I had no motivation to cook), where we talked and laughed with Nick. He still looked healthy and robust, and not at all consumed with fear, like I was.

The transition continued with blessings through email, phone messages, and sleep. The next morning, some wonderful ladies encouraged me to go to my Thursday morning devotional group, and my resolve continued when a friend insisted I meet her for a yoga class, and I said yes.

The day was moving along. I was feeling a little bit of my inner strength coming back. Then Nick came in from school with his big old smile and told me he talked to his teachers and it was "all cool." His teachers would work with him as he went back into aggressive treatment. Then an email arrived from our doctor. Nick's tumor markers and bone marrows were normal; the relapse was bony lesions only.

Something about that email inspired me to invite our other kids to come over for spaghetti. The house would be filled with food and family and maybe that would be enough to bring me back…maybe not all the time, or not all the way, but enough to where I would be ready to face this new reality. I had to be who Nick needed me to be, and that was definitely not a blubbering mom!

Nick spent his final weekend before starting aggressive treatment again going to visit friends at college, and snowboarding. He finally rolled in late Sunday evening, snowboard in hand, ready to resume the fight.

Transition

Back in New York, the week of medium-dose chemo was tolerable. On Friday, the doctors agreed to let Nick return home. We agreed to have his blood checked at Georgetown the next week. We hailed a cab, boarded the train, and headed for home, after a week of "work" in the big city.

There we were, back at home. Somehow, I didn't choke up when the grocery clerk asked, "How are you today?" Somehow, I was able to think of "the next round" without despair and panic. Somehow, I had a glimmer of hope.

Being back in New York had helped. A wonderful, if bizarre, sort of power is created when you are united with others facing the same situation. There is a strength that binds you together, like fibers in a strong rope. While you are always one tear away from falling apart, there is always someone there to take a moment to calm you, and lessen the loneliness.

Once we got home, Nick shaved his head. His eyes stared steadily in the mirror as the clippers moved back and forth across his head. The piles of hair left on the floor served as another reminder that he was crossing back over, yet again. It was a routine Nick was all too familiar with—but something this time stirred a level of intensity I had not seen in him for a while. He was like an animal that had been let out of a cage. He wandered around the house and then announced he "needed to drive." The old blue truck fired up and he did his neighborhood cruise, ending with a Slurpee at the 7-Eleven.

We had three weeks to navigate a new normal once again, before returning to the fight.

The surreal life continues

By February, it was becoming clear that Nick's body was getting tired of the assault of chemo. We ended up in Georgetown with low blood counts, and it took him a long time for his low blood counts to recover. No one was optimistic that he could endure more high-dose chemo. It was time to evaluate other options.

We went back to New York to try a lower dose round of therapy. We got there under the assumption that he would start a new treatment within a couple of days of our arrival. After much consideration, the team of doctors wanted Nick to have more time to recover.

This delay opened a welcome door for Nick.

A group of his friends who he rarely saw (since they were now in college) had planned a snowboarding trip to Jackson Hole, Wyoming. We were good friends with the parents, and once they heard Nick would be free, they added him to the trip! While on the train back to Virginia, we booked his tickets, and before we knew it, he was set to leave in the morning for a week of "extreme" snowboarding. Nick was bald, kind of weak, and didn't have the greatest blood counts. *But I had learned to let him go, and let him live his life in those moments when he could.* I am sure he wasn't feeling that great, but suddenly Nick was beaming, full of energy, excited about the next five days, that were also *his life.*

While I was at home awaiting the test results we had done while in New York with my stomach in knots, I got intermittent reports from Wyoming. The hills were extreme, the snow was dumping daily, and he didn't have a care in the world. In fact, he had the time of his life! Later, when his friends described how Nick attacked the hills with no fear, we were incredibly proud and glad we heard about it *after* the fact!

His ability to absolutely defy negativity, to attack challenges, and live with positivity floors me to this day.

He got home at midnight with a week of memories that would fuel him for the next treatment. He dropped his suitcase and got in his truck—he didn't even come in to say hi! I called his phone, wondering where he was. He was at a bonfire with friends. Morning came and I left to run some errands while he was still asleep. When I returned, there was a note: *Playing disc, did some homework, see ya later.*

It was just surreal...the beat of Nick's life continued to pound out with a strong cadence, despite everything. His outlook was still completely positive. There was no way he was going to miss a thing during the times he was able. Oh, how I wanted to be more like him. He made it so we would sometimes forget that he was bald, or sick, or different. Those moments were priceless.

Blessed

As winter turned to spring in 2009, the familiar sites of home nourished our spirits and helped us to believe in new hope. Over nearly four years, I had learned to sit for hours and hours in hospital rooms tolerating uncomfortable chairs, cramped spaces, and coffee in Styrofoam cups. It felt so good to be home enjoying the simple pleasure of an afghan, my sofa, and coffee from a mug. Nick enjoyed his double bed, one that didn't vibrate, move, and wasn't lined with plastic.

We had grown so tired of hospital stays.

Medical decisions were becoming more difficult at this point. Unfortunately, we had evolved to "managing disease mode" instead of "clearing disease mode." Three major hospitals were formulating the best plan for Nick. It was decided he would enter a clinical trial at Children's Hospital of Philadelphia. Once again, we were starting new routines, and another team of wonderful doctors became our lifeline, as winter moved into spring.

During Easter service, a story was told about a license plate with a handicap sticker on it that said "BLESSED 2." The message was, despite being disabled, a person could still claim their life as blessed. I thought about that, and tried to embrace that perspective. I reminded myself how blessed I was to have an awesome family, adorable grandkids, both of my parents still alive. How blessed I was to have Nick, hiding eggs for the little ones and looking wonderful. Nick, alive, building the story of his life. Nick, who never said, "Why me," or, "I wish I had."

Nick, embracing each and every good day he could, teaching us all the lessons of his tattoo.

When I looked at my life that way, I felt "Blessed2."

The Dress Shirt

When Nick was little, I could never have imagined the perspective I now had about what a "nice day" could mean. One day in Philadelphia, that nice day included, "deaccessing" a port from my son's chest, watching him lay perfectly still during a nuclear scan, and getting him measured for a dress shirt with a hospital bracelet on. Before cancer, that description would have made my stomach churn, and knowing me, I would have thrown up! Yet, that was my reality as we adapted to our new surroundings in Philadelphia. The new clinical trial required Nick to remain in isolation for three days in a lead room. As we got him ready, there was one more task to accomplish. We needed to get Nick a dress shirt and tie to wear to a funeral for one of his friends.

Nick's friend, a perfectly healthy young man, came home from college for the weekend and dropped dead of a heart attack. It took my breath away to think of the shock and pain his family felt. We had been fighting daily for Nick's life for almost four years. In our vacuum, it was easy to forget that there are accidents, and other illnesses and tragedies that take young people suddenly. Nick's perfectly "healthy" friend was gone, and yet, Nick was not.

Life is a mystery.

With his hospital bracelet on, Nick entered a men's store in downtown Philadelphia. A very nice clerk measured him and commented on his tall but very thin build. Then he saw the hospital bracelet, and the conversation turned to Nick's story, and his reason for buying the shirt. As we left, we realized what an impact those few moments had on the clerk. He looked Nick in the eye and sincerely shared how moved he was by Nick's story. He vowed to pray for us and for the family who lost their son.

Through sadness, grief, and fear, we made a new "heart" connection, and we carried on. It was a "nice day."

He was able to complete the clinical trial in a lead lined room and return to school with very few side effects. Plans were made to celebrate his high-school graduation, a day I feared would never come.

Nick's Walk

For nearly four years, Nick had been walking a unique path. It was a path no one could understand, unless they lived it. His walk took him in and out of so many exam rooms, IV rooms, operating rooms, treatment rooms, ICU rooms, and inpatient rooms. He was forced to walk into so many unknown and scary situations, time after time. He had become intimately familiar with chest ports, IV placements, chemo drips, blood transfusions, painful antibody treatments, radiation therapy, nuclear scans, and bone-marrow biopsies.

He walked a path where he was constantly aware that his life was in danger. He walked into rooms where his normal teenage life was ripped away, again and again, with just one scan, one phone call, one sentence. Each time that his anger swelled he walked away, cooled down, and accepted what fate brought him. He bravely walked straight into whatever was asked of him, with acceptance, grace, and dignity. He walked in and out of school, always a step behind, enduring isolation, separation, and humiliation.

All of that made it so very much more meaningful and powerful, when Nick walked across the stage and accepted his high-school diploma. He didn't want to stand out in the sea of five hundred caps and gowns. While many kids seek out special recognition, Nick turned down the invitation to be the senior commencement speaker. He wanted to be just one of the crowd—because being just like everyone else was the greatest gift of all.

When Nick's name was called, just like everyone else's, our hearts soared, we clapped with pride. He shook hands, accepted his diploma, and walked back to his seat, ready to walk into his future.

Like the song said, he continued walking the line between faith and fear, with his head held high.

Nick: In His Own Words

College Essay

My Life, by Nick Franca

Growing up and maturing into an adult is a normal rite of passage. For most everybody, it comes naturally. Some, such as myself, are forced to grow up and make life changing decisions earlier than expected. My life as I knew it disappeared forever the summer after my freshman year.

I was fifteen. I had a normal childhood, nothing wrong, no problems with other kids, and I really faced no hardships. When I was fourteen, I moved and was going to a new high school. I was having a great time and had a lot of friends. During final exam week of freshman year, I had an appendicitis attack. The emergency room doctor performed surgery and discovered a small "cyst" on my spine. I was to get a CAT scan to check it out.

About halfway through the summer, I got my CAT scan, and the scan showed more than a small cyst on my spine. Over the course of that summer, I went through multiple scans and tests, all of which were not looking good. I didn't think anything of the whole situation, but I could see that it was hurting my parents.

At the end of July, I finally had a needle biopsy of the tumor. The results of the biopsy looked promising. They came back as benign, but the team of doctors still wanted to take the mass out of my back. In mid-August, after multiple consults with surgeons, I went in for the resection. The surgeons' plan was to go in through my stomach and then flip me over and perform a type of surgery where they lift off my spine. Eleven hours later, they were done. The next day, the doctors came in and told my family that the operation was a success, and that there were no cancerous spots.

Later that day they came back in and gave us the news that my bone marrow was packed with neuroblastoma—a rare cancer of the sympathetic nervous system.

We were shocked, of course, but so were the doctors because neuroblastoma is most common in kids five and under. It is very rare in teens. And I had had no symptoms at all.

My sophomore year was to start in two weeks, and I had even tried out for the golf team just before the surgery. Instead, my family took me to New York City, and I became a resident of the Ronald McDonald House, five blocks from Memorial Sloan Kettering Cancer Center. I was there for nine months. I began a horrible and aggressive treatment for Stage 4 neuroblastoma. I left the life I knew and now can barely remember. I had to depend on my parents for everything at a time when I wanted to begin stepping out on my own.

The news that I had cancer was taken hardest by my family. I never thought too much about it. It was just something I had to get through. But seeing my family cry and be worried was harder than dealing with the cancer itself. Letters of sorrow started pouring in from relatives, friends, and people that I had never even met before.

I tried to start my sophomore year during chemo through the cancer clinic teachers, but I soon found that the violent sickness that came with chemo and yet another surgery made that impossible. As a family, we decided to withdraw my enrollment from school. I would miss my sophomore year. My only job was to cope with the treatments.

I had no idea what to expect from chemo. Within hours of my first five-day drip, I knew this was absolute hell. I had never experienced sickness like the kind during high-dose chemo. But it didn't end with just being nauseous like I thought it would. A week later, I began to learn a different vocabulary than my friends in English class. That week my blood counts started dropping. I had no idea that this was going to happen. I also had no idea how important your blood is to you. While other kids were learning algebra and chemistry, I was learning how to read my blood count reports. I learned about platelets, red blood cells, white blood cells, absolute neutrophils, neutropenic fevers, and the importance of all these to my survival. I spent over forty days in the hospital with no white blood cells. Overall, I endured six high dose rounds of chemo. I learned to give myself shots to boost my white blood cell count and to flush the lines dangling from my chest. It was important for me to do these things without the help of my parents. I had a determination, a focus, a desire to be in control of SOMETHING, even if it was only injecting myself and changing my own port dressings. I got to visit home a couple of times, and even went to a football game, bald and pale. I lost 35 pounds; for me, that was a lot.

After nine months of high dose chemo, I was declared NED (no evidence of disease). After I was declared cancer free, I still had to go through treatment. No more chemo, but I had to do antibody treatment and radiation, For the next year, I received the antibodies. Antibody treatments affect the nerve cells in the body, and I had to learn to cope with pain that I can only describe as bone crushing. Many of the parents looked to me to explain what their little ones felt. I was old enough to articulate how painful the treatment was. Their young children could just scream. The pain is so intense that you get pain "rescues" until you pass out and try to sleep it off. I started the antibody treatment the summer of 2006 and planned on starting back to school in the fall. I knew school would be hard because antibody treatments were a week long every three weeks. I would gain a few pounds and then lose them again during the antibody cycles.

September came, and I was enrolled in my sophomore year in high school, a year behind where I would have been if cancer had not altered my plans. I knew I had to maintain my grades and still do my treatments. Not many people in my grade knew who I was because I was not there the year before. Explaining my situation to them was always tough because I did not want people to think of me as different. When I walked through the doors of high school, I wanted desperately to be normal. I missed a lot of school that year, one week a month. But one good thing about antibody treatment, when it's over, it's over. I did not have the aftereffects of chemo. I managed to make new friends in my new grade. I was able to maintain decent grades, even though it was tough.

At the end of my sophomore year, I went to New York for routine scans, all of which were good except for one, which showed two new spots on my hip and spine. So the doctors collaborated and made the decision to put me back on chemo. The chemo they decided on was relatively easy, but it still lowered my counts and made me sick.

My junior year came, and once again I missed school one week out of four for my chemo cycle. Everyone junior year was focusing on college prep. I was focused on surviving, and balancing treatment with school and teenage life. I could only take basic classes and endured another major surgery for adhesions. I spent another twenty days in the hospital recovering from a bowel obstruction. My grades dropped a little from the year before. I tried to keep up, but being out of school almost as much as being in school was difficult. But I got through my junior year, somehow balancing my two lives.

I am still doing the chemo once every three weeks. But this summer I worked at the summer camp I began attending as a child. I was a leader and a role model for young children as their counselor. I was bald and thin when I arrived after a particularly rough treatment in the spring. In the six weeks I lived there, I had to drive myself home for a week-long treatment once, and every weekend I had to drive to the local hospital and get my blood counts checked. I am eighteen, and I've learned responsibility for myself. My childhood ended abruptly three years ago, but one of the gifts is my ability to cope with the things I have to do to stay alive.

People say I have a wisdom about me. People say I am brave. People say they can't imagine what fears I must have and how I keep going. I have just always assumed I will keep going. No one knows how they will react if given the news I got three years ago. My attitude has always been to look to the future and not dwell on the horror I sometimes live.

Now it is time to go to college. Much as I would love to, I don't have the typical profile of a prospective college candidate. But I have learned about life.

Determination, optimism, and perseverance are important life skills that will surely play a role in how I approach and handle college. My life is a gift. I am here, and I want the chance to have a future through my college education.

Beach Week

I truly couldn't believe that, with all the challenges his senior year brought, my son had graduated from high school and been accepted to college. Nick, however, did believe it—and the celebration continued as he headed to "beach week" in Myrtle Beach. He returned a week later with no apparent new tattoos or piercings, he wasn't too sunburned, he wasn't too exhausted. He was just happy.

He became an uncle again, and my daughter chose Nicholas as the middle name of her second son, Jackson. Nick went to the hospital and held his namesake before packing for college orientation the next day.

There was no stopping him. He was focused on his goal, and everything was falling into place. The treatment he was on now was very tolerable. He had hair, he had gained some weight, and he had hope again. After orientation, he would head to Camp Varsity again to be a counselor for a few weeks.

I marveled at my son. Watching him drive away once again, I imagined him posting an online ad for a job. It would read:

Nineteen-year-old male, been through hell for four years battling a rare cancer, contracted at the wrong age. Desperately seeking a normal life with catch-up time for the years missed. Looking for any and all free time away from reminders that there still may be cancer lingering in his body, including family dinners where the conversation would stay in the present moment, not the looming scans in July.

After orientation and two weeks as a counselor, he would be facing the reality of scans again. This time we would go to Philadelphia, where he was in the clinical trial...that would, hopefully, still be working.

A Summer Day

Nick's July scans weren't clean, but they showed lots of improvement. That meant he could start a new maintenance therapy which meant—and this was the truly amazing thing—he could finally go away to college in September.

Nick did *not* want to go to college with a port in his chest. His oncologist in Philadelphia agreed. So, we juggled and scheduled, and arranged to have the chest port removed. It still amazes me what we could achieve in one day when Nick was determined to accomplish a goal!

4:30 a.m.: Awake and dress to drive up the East Coast.
5:15 a.m.: Skim latte at Starbucks in Virginia.
7:45 a.m.: Pull into hospital parking garage In Philadelphia, two and a half hours from home.
8:00 a.m.: Check into surgery reception…go to cubicle for preparation. Sign consents, start IV, talk to surgeon, anesthesia.
11:15 a.m.: Begin surgery to remove chest port.
12:15 p.m.: Recovery room…wake up from surgery; eat lunch. The nurse commented that most kids want ginger ale, saltines, and a popsicle. I told her we have been doing surgeries for four years…we go for the nine-inch subs after "nothing by mouth" since midnight!
2:00 p.m.: Fully recovered, dressed. Nurse leaves to get a wheelchair to take Nick to the oncology clinic. She returns to find Nick standing up, fully dressed—no wheelchair for him!
2:30 p.m.: Go over all the rules and regulations of our next clinical trial. Take the first dose.
3:15 p.m.: In the car, head south toward Washington. Hit DC rush hour.
7:00 p.m.: *Home.*

Goal accomplished! Nick no longer had the port. He was able to move to the new trial with even fewer side effects because his scans were good. Once home, he took the three pills for the new trial with no problem. Despite the fact that his shoulder was very sore where the port was removed, Nick hopped on the computer, made a few plans, and headed out the door to go shopping in preparation for another couple weeks of Camp Varsity as a counselor. Later, he would meet up with his college roommate to discuss "stuff."

He had stitches, he had surgical glue, and he had pain, *but* he had *hope*!

I rested on the couch exhausted, but with a little of that hope too.

A New Pair of Shoes

First day of college

Another miraculous day was upon us. Jim and I drove Nick to college and left him there. Through all the setbacks, he never wavered in his determination to accomplish this goal. Our beautiful boy went away to school.

Before we left for that miraculous journey, I noticed a pile of stuff Nick was leaving behind, sitting by my office door. For some reason, I was drawn to the pile of old shoes. Some of those shoes had guided Nick up and down First

Avenue, leading him to treatments that gave him hope. Some shoes never had been worn because he had been too weak to get dressed for long periods of time, and lived in slippers.

At 9:00 a.m. on that day, the class of 2013 marched on to the beautiful green lawn to be received by the college during the convocation. Again, I noticed the shoes. In the sea of students, I spotted Nick...he didn't have his ratty black flip flops on, he was wearing a shiny new pair of white tennis shoes. The whole thing struck me—*A new pair of shoes for a new chapter in life.*

The convocation speakers spoke of "just doing it" and taking chances, and believing in yourself and persevering when times seemed challenging. I looked at the kids and I thought to myself, *No one...not one person sitting here on their first day of college has walked in Nick's shoes.* Maybe some had suffered, had hardship, struggled with disease...I didn't really know. What I did know was that the message those students heard on their first morning of college was one Nick had already learned. His high-school years were anything but normal. He didn't even attend a good part of the time, but he certainly knew how to "just do it." He knew how to persevere.

The speakers went on, talking about "the next four years." For a brief moment, I was caught up in the speech. I forgot, just for a moment, that we didn't measure time in years, we measured time in-between scans. We lived for short-term goals. The idea of lofty, four-year goals was too much to handle. And yet, Nick sat with the rest of the freshman class, seeing himself in the shoes they described. For that one hour, he was just one of the many new students, with a new pair of shoes, and with new hopes and dreams.

My Inner Compass

With Nick away at college, I planned a much-needed escape—a golf trip with my girlfriends. Before I left for my trip, he called home, saying he was having stomach issues. It was one of the expected side effects of his therapy, so I left for my trip and tried not to worry. Of course, I was the only person on the golf course with a cell phone in their pocket instead of a golf tee. And sure enough, the phone rang. Nick had driven himself home from college in horrific pain, and he was being rushed to Georgetown Hospital.

Where does the necessary strength come from? I suddenly felt like I could collapse right there on the course. I had to focus on getting home. I hadn't driven, so one of the girls volunteered to drive me back. Once home, I had another hour's drive into Georgetown. The whole way I tried to refocus my inner core, to prepare for one of several crippling decisions Nick could be facing.

It made Nick angry and emotional when I was afraid, so I had to keep my own emotions under control. I was able to appear calm when I arrived at the hospital. I walked into his room; he was pale, weak, and mad. I immediately adopted the posture of a mother not at all in panic mode despite probable surgery for a bowel obstruction. By night, it turned out there was no reason to panic. A small bowel obstruction began to resolve, and by morning, they told Nick to go home, rest for a couple of days, and then he could return to school.

All the thoughts of possible horrible scenarios subsided and we walked out of the hospital together.

Once again, my inner compass had lost direction. For two days, my mind and body had prepared for something horrible. I had every physical manifestation, including teeth chattering and not being able to eat. Then, that same inner compass was able to reset and show me another new path. Our life steadied again, and Nick navigated his way back down the road to school, with his eyes and his heart focused on better days ahead.

New Year's Day, 2010

I spent the Christmas holidays trying hard to enjoy my real "present"—which was all about living in the present. I enjoyed friends, family, and all the normalcy that surrounded the season. Everyone was talking about how the first decade of the twenty-first century hadn't been the greatest…there was 9/11, the economic crisis, and natural disasters. For me, that all was compounded by the horror of discovering that my child had a relentless cancer that completely consumed our hearts and minds for the final four and a half years of that first decade. The bitterness, the questioning, and the utter loss of everything normal left me with a different perspective as I entered a new decade. I tried hard to look forward with positive expectations…with hope and belief. I had to.

The previous year had started with a wonderful family ski trip where Nick looked as healthy and strong as he ever had. But just one week later, we learned he had horrific disease progression. All year long we fought and fought, until we found a treatment that gave us hope. On New Year's Day 2010, I looked back on the previous year, a year where our darkness turned to light, and our despair turned to hope. From the devastation of aggressive relapse to the triumph of high-school graduation; from the uncertainty of post-high-school life, to the celebration of Nick's first semester college grades. I got exhausted just thinking about what we all, but especially Nick, had endured. But in the end, I knew we had witnessed a miracle. That was what I wanted to hold on to, as our relentless journey continued.

A dear family's son fought hard and lost his battle in January of the New Year. It was a reminder of just how fragile good days and months are. After attending his funeral, I wrote these thoughts.

What I know
I go to funerals with small caskets too often.
I stare at the front row in the church and pray we never have to sit there.
I see sorrow in the eyes of my friends who are grieving the loss of their babies.
I cry easily.
I am amazed at the poise and strength of grieving parents.
My husband's hand gives me strength as we both wipe our eyes.
Snow-covered grave sites make the sadness more intense somehow.
Listening to mass in Spanish still evokes emotion, even without translation.
LOVE is all we have.
I can't stop trying to contribute to an answer.
I do my best.
I am blessed to have so many friends and family on this journey.

The start of a new decade also meant a new set of scans. As usual, I was already nervous thinking about those agonizing twenty-four hours, waiting for results. Thoughts painfully slow danced through my mind in the night, haunting me as I tried to rest and sleep. Visualizing the doctor walking into the room with Nick's results, and fate in his hands, was an inner battle I tried to keep private. Meanwhile, Nick was packed to spend the night with friends before heading out early in the morning for a snowboarding day trip.

My nerves were for me to own. Nick just kept on loving life, not stopping to think, and not allowing one shred of doubt to enter his head.

VI
Love

The Compass Points of Friendship, Strength and Courage
Through friendship sometimes love blooms. Although circumstances may seem impossible, the loyalty and unconditional love that humans offer can shine light and hope even in the darkest of times. Learning to be the type of partner and friend that "shows up" takes strength and courage. Experience the messiness of life, it adds humility and a compassion to the soul.

Happy Anniversary

At the altar, you look into the eyes of the man who will be the father of your children and you pledge for better for worse, for richer for poorer, in sickness and in health. Those words crumble and faith is lost in so many marriages. We always tried to show our children that perseverance and small things celebrated weave together to make families strong.

I remember one anniversary when Nick was about ten. We lived at the top of a hill, and I could see to the bottom through the trees. I watched the bus pull up. A few minutes later, I realized Nick was not walking up the driveway. I waited and then started to worry a bit. After about fifteen minutes, I got in the car and drove down the driveway. I looked down the street and saw him walking toward home. When he saw my car, he hid something behind his back. As he approached the car, his beautiful smile melted any irritation I was feeling. From behind his back, he revealed a red rose surrounded by baby's breath, wrapped in green tissue with a ribbon. He had walked a block to the little flower shop in town and purchased that rose for me. He smiled that smile of his and said, "Happy Anniversary."

Little things, they feed the soul and nourish the heart.

Love, a Cookie, and the Moon

In February 2010, Nick experienced another miracle. He found love. A beautiful, strong-yet-fragile angel named Kelliann came into his life. My heart filled with joy for him.

The previous Valentine's Day, we were inpatient at Georgetown Hospital, recovering from relapse chemo and trying to harvest stem cells so Nick would have possibilities for future treatments. That day was dark and filled with uncertainty, but we got our miracle. A few weeks later he harvested stem cells. Because of that miracle, Nick became eligible for a clinical trial. Because of that clinical trial, he was able to go to college. Because he went to college, he finally had some sense of freedom. Because of that sense of freedom, he was finally able to open his heart and enjoy what twenty-year-old men should enjoy—a girlfriend, freedom from my constant hovering, and a new sense of self.

He gave Kelliann a huge decorated cookie for Valentine's Day. *It's the little things that help love grow.*

Nick had another set of scans shortly after Valentine's Day, and the results were good. That meant Nick had more time to enjoy college, love, family, and friends. After driving three hours home from scans, Jim and I dropped Nick off to see his Kelliann. As he walked to her door, Jim and I noticed the moon. It was a perfect smile, radiating from the sky. We squeezed hands, and I said, "God is smiling."

Blitzen and Panic

For Nick's fifth birthday, he got a kitten and named him Blitzen. After his next set of scans in Philadelphia, Nick went back to college. Blitzen got very sick, and we learned that we had to put him down. Nick knew that the day was coming and gave me permission to go ahead. I went to the vet to discuss the option and prepare for the procedure. I was sitting, waiting to talk with the vet when my phone suddenly rang. It was Dr. Maris—the doctor in charge of Nick's treatment in Philadelphia.

Why would he be calling me? We had been told Nick's scans looked good just one week before.

I started to panic. *Nick is back in school. We need to put our cat to sleep. Please, no more bad news.* But it was bad news. A urine marker was elevated—Nick never had that tumor marker elevated before. We never thought about the urine test we did every three months, which takes a week to get results for. His tumor markers had never expressed in that test, until then.

The doctor wanted a repeat test. My head was spinning. I could hardly focus on the vet and the cat. I don't remember driving home. Another week passed, and Nick submitted another urine test. The results were worse. His blood work was now also abnormal. Nick's liver enzymes were elevated, and he was having high blood pressure issues. We were summoned to Philadelphia for emergency scans.

Nick told Kelliann not to worry. He would be fine. He drove three hours home from school, and we then drove three more hours to Philadelphia. The silence between us was deafening. Fear seared our hearts.

The results were our worst nightmare. Nick had disease everywhere. His blood pressure was so high they had to admit him to the hospital.

One of the very darkest periods of our journey was about to begin.

Nick beat the walls of the cage he suddenly was trapped in. A dorm room the day before had turned into a hospital room and horrific news. A social worker tried to calm him down. We were asked to consider if we wanted to continue treatment at all. We consulted with our New York doctors and decided that after Nick was stabilized, we would return to New York. We would use those harvested stem cells to help him recover from another aggressive treatment. He was angry but not ready to give up.

We were transported via medical transport to Sloan Kettering, our heads spinning, our hopes diminishing, our hearts breaking.

Friends and Family, Please Hold Us Up

I vividly remember feeling lost at sea, being pulled constantly under. I pleaded to friends the following:

> *We have prayed. We have asked for Nick to have a chance to have a life. None of this has been answered. I'm in such a low point about what to even ask for, so I ask all of you who are stronger than me right now to storm the heavens in our name...for I am so weak and sad and tired that I can't even pray.*

Numb, scared, and navigating a horrible new reality, Nick now had Kelliann by his side. She had been thrust from the giddy feeling of new love to the intensity of life in a place the rest of us knew all too well—the pediatric-cancer wing of Sloan Kettering Hospital in New York City.

Kelliann was just shy of twenty years old when she reconnected with Nick during that Christmas holiday. The attraction was instant, and they picked up a fast and furious relationship. They had been friends at Camp Varsity four years earlier, which was a beautiful layer to the now-budding romance.

She knew that her new boyfriend had "battled cancer," but he never talked about it, so she assumed all was fine. They spent the winter falling in love and spent an awesome spring break together. Then her new boyfriend headed to Philadelphia for a routine scan for that cancer that he'd battled in the past...and everything fell apart.

Now, Kelliann was witness to the nightmare we had seen so many times before—"aggressive cancer treatment." For the first time in her life, she was in a cancer hospital, with the IV poles attached to multiple machines, the bald babies, and shell-shocked parents. Over those first few days, she saw her strong, healthy boyfriend transformed into an exhausted, sick patient battling a very dangerous disease.

But Kelliann was Kelliann. She reached out to all the little kids in the hospital. She played with them and made signs for their rooms. Some people asked her if she was a child life specialist. She learned to sit for hours and watch the suffering. She learned to navigate New York City on her own, and to live at the Ronald McDonald House, and to connect with total strangers.

I, on the other hand, felt void of emotion as we moved through the unthinkable. I worried about Kelliann and what she would be able to handle. She had trouble with her nerves and got sick easily. Nick tried to step in to protect her, while still struggling with his own physical and emotional challenges.

The three of us made for a tragic and tender scene. I slowly stepped back and allowed the two of them to nurture each other through the hours and the days. Through it all, I felt lost. I no longer knew who I was in this mess. What I did know was that their love was stronger than disease. Their intense desire to weather this storm side by side filled my heart, which, at the same time, was slowly breaking.

Courage, Love, and Friendship

Kelliann did not leave Nick's side for eleven days. He had massive complications from the treatment, including a bleeding bladder and bowel obstruction. When he was curled up in a fetal position on a stretcher being rushed to x-ray, she marched right beside him, along with his other angel, and dear friend, Michael Brown. She didn't have to do it. But after getting to know her very quickly, I realized that, for Kelliann, there was no other option. She had Nick's heart and he had hers. When I saw her squeezing his wart-infested hands (another tragic side effect of a compromised immune system) and stroking his arm as he suffered through the pain, I knew my son and his girl had known each other for a lifetime, on some level.

When she returned home, Kelliann finally got the courage to read Nick's entire story, from when he was first diagnosed in 2005, through that moment. After she finished, she wrote this to me:

> *All I can say is I have never seen so many friends, family and even strangers rallying to support you all. Every bit counts and it is beautiful. I am so grateful and lucky to get the opportunity to help the Franca family and especially Nick in ANY way possible. Nick is my angel and I pray to God that I can be his. The past eleven days spent with you Caryn, and Nick, I cannot even begin to describe why and how I know everything will be okay. The positive energy that surrounds your family is overwhelming to me and has helped me cope in so many ways. The phrase, "Why do bad things happen to good people?" is all I replay in my mind. Then I think well, God gives us obstacles that we must learn to tackle and everything does happen for a reason, right? The things we are put through only make us stronger, wiser, better people in the end...that's what we must live by.*

Nicholas Toms, you are truly an angel to me. I am so lucky to have found someone so considerate, thoughtful, loving, funny, mature, sexy, intelligent, and nerdy (ha ha). I could go on and on. Your courage, strength, wisdom, and attitude telling me constantly: "This is what I have to do babe, I'll be fine" is what has gotten you this far. You never give up and you always have a smile on your face, even when you are in wrenching pain, just to make sure the other person knows that you care. You have such a beautiful soul and so many friends praying for you and supporting you. It's unbelievable to me that I got so lucky to be with someone who literally takes my breath away. You are a true hero to so many and will continue to be to me forever.

Easter 2010—A Palm Branch, the Love of a Brother, and Eggs

Easter was approaching, the season of new beginnings. I so wanted to believe that we were moving in the direction of hope—but Palm Sunday passed and Nick remained in the hospital with post chemo complications. His surgeon took the time to bring a palm branch to his bedside after he attended services. That gesture touched us all.

The next week was challenging, filled with bowel obstruction pain and overall weakness. My son Jeff arrived for Easter weekend. Since Nick loved to color eggs, I got a project ready and we planned to spend the afternoon hanging out with him trying to make the most of the day. But the post chemo fever didn't hold off just because it was Easter. By early afternoon, the fever and shaking had started. For two hours, I watched as Jeff climbed in bed with his brother and laid his body on Nick's, trying to calm his shaking.

Jeff was great with Nick. The intense love they shared was so moving. As the nurses worked to get Nick safe and comfortable, Jeff had to say good-bye. Later, Nick woke up from a deep sleep and I glanced over at the shopping bag filled with Easter eggs and decorations. I knew it wasn't a good idea to even bring it up. Instead, we turned on the TV and held hands, and I stroked my son's beautiful head and whispered how much I loved him.

I missed my grandchildren and my big Easter dinners and eggs hunts at my house. I missed Jim, my parents, my brother, daughter, grandkids, and the rest of my family. Nick and I were there alone, trying to feel like it was Easter, but the only evidence was an unopened bag of plastic eggs and a faded palm branch.

Living Like Nick Does—My Inspiration

The treatment and complications further deepened the crater we felt ourselves falling into. Days and nights blurred. Nick's misery broke our hearts, yet he didn't complain beyond the infrequent cuss word and frequent statement that this just *sucked.*

Winter had turned to spring and support swelled like a rising river of love. Blood and platelets flowed into our bank—as valuable as rubies and gold. One night I noticed white blossoms on the trees above me, as I walked the streets of New York. They seemed to be a hint of new life, of hope.

Finally, we returned home. As we lumbered south on Amtrak, tulip blossoms and daffodils rushed by us in a blur of color. Our winter of dread had given way to a spring of hope. Hope that we had time. Hope that we had options.

Home was vivid with the colors of spring. A pot roast simmered in the crock pot, brought by a friend. Nick ate well but also shaved his head—a reminder of the reality that we were back in fight mode.

Once again, we had been knocked completely off-kilter. The medical routine that dictated the rhythm of our life for the past four weeks had again given way to life at home. How was I supposed to do "home"? All the familiar things felt out of step. How was I supposed to jump back into a life I barely remembered? An emotional blur enveloped me like a thick, cold fog.

Then I watched Nick. Nick texting friends. Nick making plans with Kelliann. Nick soaking in the peace of home.

Nick living his life.

Step by step, we carved out a new normal once again. By Thursday night we were enjoying another fabulous meal, brought by another friend. Nick had a couple of friends over to just hang out for a while.

Nick went to the clinic at Georgetown by himself, got platelets, and then hung out with his brother Jeff for the afternoon. That afternoon found me on the golf course for the first time in a long time, followed by dinner with friends.

That was how we did it. We just plunged back into normal life and let the love of others help us get into the flow.

One of my hardest moments was saying good-bye to Nick before he drove the three hours to Lynchburg College. He would not be staying at school. Instead, he would be packing up his room and saying good-bye to college. My heart broke watching him let go of that dream. He wanted to do it without us, and we let him.

Through it all, I struggled to be as brave as Nick was. Five years in, I was still learning, still growing, watching how Nick navigated the hand he had been dealt. I asked myself all the time, "What would Nick do"? Then, I would find myself getting off the couch, out of bed, out of my mental funk and embracing the life I had that day.

Because isn't that really all any of us have?

VII
New Hope

The Compass Point of Courage

To be brave in the midst of the inevitable seems like an impossible task. Nick had always believed he wasn't going to die. But one day, he softly said to me, "Please help me live five more years."

Courage means staying focused on a goal in the midst of chaos. It means digging deeper than you ever had to dig, just to find moments of calm and peace. Nick's courage radiated as he tried to live a normal existence, while facing difficult medical challenges that consumed his days. A walk, a dinner with friends, a game of Frisbee golf, a conversation with a young pastor. These touchstones fed his courage, as disease and time battled one another. His courage served him, but it also emanated to those around him.

Just when we thought we were out of options, hope appeared again. After the round of high-dose chemotherapy and an exhausting, long recovery, we got positive news from our hospital in Philadelphia. They had tested Nick's bone marrow and found a genetic mutation that made him eligible for a new clinical trial. This trial was very tolerable, with oral drugs that blocked the mutation of the gene, at least that was the theory.

A Walk across Campus and a White Dove

Nick's new trial at Children's Hospital in Philadelphia was next to a university. We wound up wheeling our suitcases from the hotel to the hospital in the middle of all the college students walking to class. Their hurried steps, their eyes cast forward, focusing on their next project or test, was similar to our walk, but we had a very different goal in mind.

Nick just wanted to live; that's all.

As we left the hospital to board the train to Virginia, Jim called. He was fishing in our pond at sunset. Usually geese and crows fly by, but that night, out of nowhere, a single, pure white dove circled around the pond. It flew around for a few minutes and then landed and sat on the dam next to him. It cocked its head and looked at Jim for a minute and then flew away. It was like a whisper from spirit that we were, at the moment, okay.

Summer 2010

The clinical trial in Philadelphia was going well. Scans showed stable disease, but Nick developed another bowel obstruction that required hospitalization at Georgetown. All of the radiation he had to his abdomen and spine made bowel obstructions one of our biggest threats.

The frustration of being imprisoned in a body that would not cooperate was difficult. As the days went by, our wonderful doctor, Dr. Gonzales, was able to slowly ease the obstruction without surgery. June was ticking by...and Kelliann never left his side.

A Vacation and a Terrifying Homecoming

Kelliann's parents owned a condominium at Atlantis in the Bahamas, and they offered it to Nick and Kelliann for a vacation in July. Miraculously, Dr. Gonzales was able to discharge Nick and encouraged him to go on his trip. Kelliann and

Nick arrived at our house from the hospital at ten at night. They were due to fly out the next morning. Getting to the airport was challenging, but they made it, and while I was relieved, I was also nervous.

The week came and went and they had a blast...or so I thought.

Later, I found out the real story.

They had missed their first flight home, and when I spotted them finally walking through security at the airport I could tell something was very wrong. Nick was not feeling well—he told us he had a headache and abdominal pain. We were scheduled to go to Philadelphia the next day for his check-up, but when Nick got in the car he quietly said "Dad, I can't make it, take me to Georgetown now." Hearing the desperation in Nick's voice, Jim immediately changed his route.

About two blocks from the hospital, Nick had a violent seizure. When the convulsing subsided, he was not breathing. Kelliann started CPR in the back seat and got him breathing again, but he was disoriented and agitated. When we pulled up to the emergency room, they took Nick back to work on him. I did what I always did. I threw up and started convulsing.

My daughter arrived and helped calm me down, but we soon learned the news was not good. Nick's disease had exploded once again. His brain seizure was caused by blood pressure that was extremely high, and he was close to a stroke.

I was terrified, again, that we would lose him.

Once Nick was stabilized, we were transported by ambulance to Philadelphia, where Nick was pulled from the trial we had placed so much hope in. We were left with only one, final option. Go back to New York and hit the disease hard, one more time.

"You Could Milk a Cow"

For the better part of the next four months, we lived full time in New York. Nick's body was weak and complications from treatment meant we were constantly in and out of the hospital. Kelliann stayed with us for most of the fall. The slow and difficult acceptance of letting go of control sunk deep into my soul.

But Nick still had such a desire to live.

The most challenging complication from this round of chemo was damage to Nick's bladder that caused it to hemorrhage. A Foley catheter saline flush became a common occurrence. For most young men of almost twenty-one, having their most private of parts hooked up to drainage tubes, tended by nurses, would be devastating. But Nick being Nick took it in stride—*just another part of accepting what he could not change.*

One night, one of his favorite nurses was squatting on a stool by his bed, working to squeeze and drain the Foley bag. Nick looked down at her and said, "You'd be good at milking a cow." Typical Nick, always trying to be entertaining and kind, trying to ease the drama and lessen the tragedy of the situation.

A Caramel Cake and a Special Rice Krispie Treat

In the middle of the horror of Foley catheters malfunctioning, and sub-pubic tubes needing to be aspirated, and chemo and complications and general awfulness, Nick made it to his twenty-first birthday. We had a glass-half-full kind of celebration.

First came an amazing surprise visitor. The teacher who was Nick's biggest source of support in getting through high school left her twenty-month-old baby behind, drove five hours, and walked into his hospital room with twenty-one balloons and birthday gifts. I was moved to tears.

Next, four of Nick's friends came up from Virginia on the train, donated platelets, and hung out. Nick's brother Jeff and sister Alyson arrived, and there were more tears of reunion. Then Nick's great friend Michael Brown arrived with a homemade caramel cake—Nick's favorite. (Michael's mom still makes a caramel cake on Nick's birthday each year.) There were visits from Kelliann's parents, and by five that night he was exhausted. He would be starting chemo the next day—his last hope of living just a little bit longer.

There was also a special surprise hidden in the bounty of gifts and treats that arrived for his birthday. Someone had delivered a "special batch" of Rice Krispie treats, made with medical marijuana that was supposed to help with nausea. Being the mom I am, I agreed to try one with him, for his birthday.

Little did I know the effect it would have on me. While Nick had an incredibly high tolerance for drugs from all he had been through, my experience was not so good. At least Nick got a laugh out of watching his stoned, freaked out mother saying, "I am done now, make it stop!"

At some point during my "experience," Nick's bladder catheter came dislodged. I don't know how it happened, but suddenly I looked up and saw white coats hovering over his bed. I of course, freaked. I definitely wasn't the "mom" in charge with my very buzzed brain! I ended up throwing up, at which point my daughter and Nick burst out laughing. The surgical team, with no clue why I was so out of it, got concerned about me.

My daughter deadpanned, "I think it was something she ate." The doctors asked if I wanted to go get checked out…OMG, no, I did *not*!

That was Nick's twenty-first and last birthday on earth. He spent it surrounded by family and friends and ended the day laughing his head off at his stoned mother, who was just trying to be part of the party!

It was a good day.

Home Again

After months of treatment and complications in New York, Nick returned to Virginia in January 2011. We spent Christmas and New Year's Eve with him in the hospital. He was clearly weaker but his resolve was stronger than ever. His new treatment consisted of a pill that had few side effects, and we hoped that would keep him stable long enough for the long-awaited opening of the fully funded Band of Parents antibody trial.

The Key

Amid the many cards that Nick received for his birthday and Christmas, one served a special purpose. It was a motivator. It helped Nick set a goal. It was also an amazing gesture and the magnitude of what it represented was probably not even realized at the time.

Inside of a card was a gift from family friends back home. Their son was one of Nick's inner circle of friends. Inside the card was the key to their amazing beach house in Sandbridge, Virginia.

When Nick held that key in his hand, it represented the possibility of something to look forward to, and an escape from the misery he was living at the time. He fantasized about surprising Kelliann with a New Year's Eve getaway. That didn't happen. He was still inpatient when New Year's rolled around. So he kept the key in his wallet and reset his goal.

That key represented release from the hospital walls that had become his cage. Nick was like an animal in the zoo…he patiently tolerated his hospital environment, appreciating the care and nurturing he got. But the minute he was released to the "wild" of his normal life, he shut and locked that memory in a separate cage in his mind.

There could be no more fitting gift for Nick than that key. For him, the key to living life was to always have the drive and focus to reset his course. He needed to be working toward something in the "real" world. The key to his ability to tolerate the suffering, pain, humiliation, and isolation that were such a dominant part of his life was his constant faith that he would have better days. Faith that the cage would open, and he would finally be released to get strong and thrive.

Since New Year's was out of the question, Nick reset his compass and decided he would surprise Kelliann for their first anniversary with "the key." He dreamed and schemed about it for a couple of weeks. He was determined to press on and make it work, even with a difficult platelet and bladder situation.

And he did.

As Nick drove four hours south to the beach with his sweetheart, it didn't matter that it was January and very cold. It didn't matter that he now had semi-permanent tubes coming from his lower abdomen to drain his bladder when it started bleeding. Nothing mattered, except getting gas in the car, and a key in the door, for a few days of freedom.

Live For Today

What an overused phrase that is! But when it came to Nick, "live for today" was his way of life. After just three weeks back home in Virginia, Nick decided to look for an apartment.

Unlike the horror and chaos of 2010, Nick was tolerating his new drug well, and he was ready to find a way to escape the constant thumb of living at home with us. This didn't exactly make sense, given his very precarious situation, but we didn't discourage him. *Setting and achieving goals kept Nick going*. The search for an apartment was complicated. Eventually, he got discouraged and began to feel like nothing was going to work out.

Once again, friends showed up and opened their hearts—like so many had, so many times.

These particular friends had a Civil War era cabin on their beautiful farm property. Over the years it had been rented, or their adult children had used it. At the time Nick was looking for his own place, it happened to be empty. Our friends offered to rent it to Nick and Kelliann on a month-to-month basis. (In reality the only rent they paid was to help with a couple of barn chores on the property.)

Such generosity.

The joy and excitement overtook all of us. Nick wasted no time. He threw all of his clothes, a DVD player, his perfect push-up device, his treatment drugs, and the daily journal he had to keep into a bunch of big, black trash bags. He slung his backpack over his shoulder and flashed his beautiful smile. It occurred to Jim and me that this was really happening.

In bed that night, we held each other and thought about Nick's tattoo, and what it meant. We marveled at how family, friends, strength, and courage, and especially faith, really were the creed our boy lived by. For however long, he would have his independence. He would live the way he wanted to.

He would Live Like Nick.

For about six weeks, he was able to manage things well. He drove to Georgetown hospital three days a week to receive platelets, as his body still had not recovered fully from his treatments. He accepted this as his job. He and Kelliann enjoyed their little cabin and their simple life.

I'll never forget the last time I saw Nick happy. In April 2011, he went to dinner with his best buddy, Michael, and his sweetheart, Kelliann. He stopped by our house for a few minutes, and he just radiated joy. He had an incredible ability to celebrate simple things, like going out with friends and having his girl by his side. To Nick, that was a good life.

Early the next morning, he woke up very sick. He called us to say he wasn't well, and he was just going to try and rest. But Jim didn't like the way Nick sounded on the phone, and later that afternoon, he went to the cabin.

When Jim arrived, Nick was limp and unresponsive. His fever had suddenly spiked to 104. He couldn't move on his own, and we couldn't move him ourselves. An ambulance was called. He was taken out of his little cabin on a stretcher, the cabin that represented his freedom and happiness.

He would never return.

At the hospital, we learned Nick's blood counts had bottomed out and he was in septic shock. For two endless weeks, we held vigil by his bedside. We played his favorite music. Friends and family sat with us. We kept hoping he would become responsive and turn a corner. He always had before.

This time that outcome was not meant to be. On May 1, 2011, Nick made his transition, leaving us all with broken hearts. But he had also left us a gift—the resilience and determination to live the lessons from his tattoo.

To Live Like Nick Did. Every day.

VIII

Now What? *Living the Compass Points*

Courage, Strength, Friends, Family, Faith
Dear Nick,
Birth and death...the circle of life.
There were times in the past two days that I felt very much like we were laboring as a family...helping you to give birth to your new life in a new dimension...the waiting, the watching the monitor, the breathing, the exhaustion...
Except this time, we were not laboring to give you life on Earth, but to give birth to eternal life where you were released from the body that was so aggravating to you. It was not your body. Your spirit busted out and spread through the world today...a joyous new birth where you can smile and navigate a new dimension in a spiritual world.

My Dearest Nicholas,

I have mixed feelings about this latest turn of events in your life. Your passing has created a chasm in my heart. I cannot yet fathom that I will not see you again, in this life. I will not fish, golf, watch football, ride the four-wheeler, go drag racing, walk the beach, learn from or teach you, ever again. You were one of my favorite companions for many activities. The loss of that companionship is devastating for me. Your courage, tenacity, drive and sense of humor in the midst of this horrendous medical battle was an honor to observe in close quarters. You

complained little, fought with grace and dignity, and never considered failure as an option. I know that I could not have done what you did. You hated to be called heroic, but you were; did not understand the admiration others had for you, but they did; you considered how you lived and battled to be what anyone would do, but it wasn't. Your efforts were superhuman, and I admired you greatly, as a man, as a son, as a patient, as a warrior. I am so proud of who you became. To be known as the father of Nick Franca is a big stuff, big, important stuff. You gave it your all, nothing held back, nothing left undone. Everyone, and I mean EVERYONE knows that. I will miss you and forever know that we have been cheated out of the remainder of our life together. So be it. I know what you want me to do about that…live fully in other ways, never feel sorry for myself and make the most of life as it has been presented, not as I think it "should" be. That is your legacy to me, and many others. Goodbye for now Nick, I will always love you with all my heart.
Dad

Over seven hundred people gathered as friends played the same song Nick shared with me during antibodies. "We're All in This Thing Together" by Old Crow Medicine Show brings me to tears, even today. Friends, family, and several ministers honored Nick with stories. After the service hundreds gathered in the same park that held a vigil six years earlier. Our town park was transformed into a beautiful venue to share stories and honor our son. *Friends and family truly are the glue that holds you together when every ounce of your being has been shattered.* We were so moved.

We buried our son that May.

The Cards

For weeks, Jim and I had been letting the cards that kept streaming in from family, friends, and even strangers pile up. Now, after the burial, a long nap, and our grandson's t-ball game, the time finally seemed right.

We were reminded, yet again, of how permanent our painful new reality was.

As a thunderstorm rumbled outside, we hunkered down on our old-but-cozy back porch. We turned on the party lights, played "jazz for a rainy afternoon," and started opening the cards. A couple of hours passed.

Reading those messages helped us to begin our healing. It felt validating to read the verses on the cards and have so many people acknowledge our pain. I was touched by the many notes that were enclosed. I learned that Nick had made a profound impact on others. Without trying to, he just did.

A classmate from Nick's high school whom we never knew wrote from Ohio:

> *Nick had a huge impact on me and really inspired me. He taught me how to live every day and live life to the fullest, not to just exist, but to live. I have heart problems and have had many heart attacks, doctors have tried different things but nothing seems to work. I am only a year younger than Nick, as I am 20. I have been going downhill lately. After a car wreck I had, he was awesome to me when I had to relearn to talk and walk. He even helped me relearn my ABCs. He really taught me how to love and how to live my life because we never know what day might be the last. Your son meant a lot to me and always will. I could never thank him enough for all that he taught and did for me. He was a real*

inspiration and had an impact on many people's lives. Without your son, I doubt I would be alive today because I would have given up. But after knowing your son and seeing him fight to the very end, I could never give up.

A dear friend and mother to one of Nick's closest friends wrote this to Nick:

You didn't judge him or ridicule him for being a little guy; rather, you had his back when others bullied him. As a mom I will forever be grateful to you for this alone.

I want to thank you for fighting when you could have given up so easily. You had no idea my amazement when I'd read a particularly daunting post about a setback, and then see you smiling on my couch the following weekend. When I would talk to Chris about your disease, he would just say "I follow Nick's lead."

Later, as night fell and the rain subsided on a day where we opened up so many gestures of love, I thought about the way Nick lived, about how, even in his darkest, most difficult moments, he went out of his way for others.

And I vowed to go out of my way…

…to love, even when it is hard,
…to make another person smile and feel a tiny bit more connected to humanity,
…to stop someone's suffering; financially, physically, emotionally, mentally,
…to LLND—Live Like Nick Did.

Letting Go

We were learning to live again, one day at a time.

We continued to experience a kaleidoscope of emotions on a daily, even hourly basis. The days ebbed and flowed like the tides. At times the emotion was so overwhelming we felt like we were being swept away in a riptide. Then there were other times when calm prevailed, and the only ripple that penetrated our hearts would be a song, a scent, or a photograph that would suddenly take our breath and fill our eyes.

I still found it impossible to go anywhere without my cell phone in my hand. For years, I had been perpetually on edge, waiting for a text, a phone call, an email. I had to be available 24-7. I had to be vulnerable 24-7, constantly living in fear of what might unfold.

It was a hard pattern to unlearn.

I fought to let go and live with one intention: to Live Like Nick Did on a daily basis. It took a lot of inner work and discipline.

But that is the way Nick did it.

How many days must he have felt the overwhelming enormity of his battle? Yet somehow, he pushed that aside to make someone laugh or feel good. How many hours must he have lain in bed at night, awake, with only his own thoughts? Yet, he always got up with a smile and a determination to make the next day the best it could be. How many thoughts did he have to suppress to have enough energy to function and to sustain and nurture relationships?

That is the way I chose, and continue to choose, to honor my son. To always ask those questions and to self-check. To ask every day, am I living like Nick did?

Living Like Nick Did means living with a generous heart and a compassion for others. He always did that. There were countless times when he would mention to me a patient, a parent, or a friend who could use a little love and support and encouraged me to reach out with him.

So now it was time to let go of the things Nick loved. His Jeep, his favorite sweatshirts, his snowboarding coat, and even his race car. Through letting them go, we also let him live on through his friends and family. We decided to keep his blue truck, and it still sits on our property to this day.

We tried to honor him by being mindful and to create meaning. His friends were moved.

A Letter to you in Heaven

Dear Nick,

It has been two weeks now since your heart stopped, and our hearts broke. As you were fighting with all you had to breathe and to open your eyes when people called your name, I remember pledging to never, ever not fight to live like you so desperately wanted to. You strained to open your eyes to see us one more time at about nine that Saturday night…six hours before you left us. Your dad called me into the room and you stared at us for a good two minutes…oh how I wish I knew what your eyes were trying to tell us. I see those eyes every night when I try to shut mine. I see those eyes every morning when mine have to open again. Now my eyes desperately look for signs of you. I am obsessed with searching for you. The more I look the less likely I am to see. I think that is the way it is now.

For just shy of 6 years I spent my life looking. I looked for the best hospitals. I looked through countless internet searches, through numerous clinical trials. My "favorites" toolbar is filled with promising studies that I was constantly looking towards, not only to help you, but others in our cancer family who were searching too. One of the lessons I am painfully aware of having to learn is that the search is over. The intense anxiety I awaken with every day is about feeling I haven't done something I should have.

I keep seeing your eyes that night…yellow from jaundice, not really focused, but so intently staring at us. Maybe they were saying, keep your eyes open to new life, Mom and Dad. I know I have to leave, but you don't. Please let my eyes become yours. Please let my spirit live on and help you see all the beauty that is still there for you on earth. Please don't waste time, please live like I did.

My sweet, sweet son…I am trying so hard to do that. My eyes are wet as I type, and I know that would make you sad. My heart beats with an empty echo…and I know that is not what you want. But I pledge this to you. Your dad and I are really, really trying to see through your eyes the way life should go on. It will just take time. Unlike all the protocols I am so used to living by, there doesn't seem to be a protocol for learning to live with a broken heart. I know all the grief cycles, and all the one day at a time stuff. We are doing that. But it isn't a printout that we check off the criteria for and make a phone call, and make a plan. Instead of the next clinical trial we are now left to move through this trial of grief…grief that blankets us so heavily that sometimes we can't move. Grief that sometimes is tucked away and we interact and function as if nothing has changed. Grief that just has to happen. Like you always said, you just have to get through it and make the best of it. That was how you lived, and now our eyes are trying to see the world like that. Our eyes are now yours, and we pledge to try and learn to look at life like you did.

So, I promise today to stop trying to force my eyes to see signs of you. I am becoming obsessed with that and it is like the watched pot that never boils. Today I will try and spend more time in gratitude that you are free and in a spiritual realm that has released you from the struggle. Then maybe I will be able to feel your whisper and see with new eyes what you are trying to teach us.
Love, Mom

Memorial Day and Natalie Merchant

Memorial Day, 2011. We went to Nick's grave for the first time since the burial. I put little flags there and kissed the ground he lay beneath. I thought about the people who missed their children who died in service to their country.

Nick loved the American flag...his friends had a special tree house that had his name and the American flag hanging on it. He dreamed of serving his country someday.

He is my hero, even though he never wanted to be called that.

Generous friends lent us a house on the water for the long weekend. We enjoyed time there with dear friends, trying to embrace the newness of what life had become.

Driving home from our getaway I had my iPod tuned to Natalie Merchant. A song that Jim and I typically connected to gratitude for one another suddenly took on a different meaning. As I drove I saw the tears dripping down Jim's cheeks...I knew he was thinking the same thing as me. No words were spoken, but we knew the words were taking on new meaning:

Kind and Generous
For your kindness I'm in debt to you
For your selflessness—my admiration
For everything you've done
You know I'm bound—I'm bound to thank you for it
You've been so kind and generous
I want to honor you and keep on giving (I changed that line a little)

For your kindness I'm in debt to you
And I never could have gone this far without you
For everything you've done
You know I'm bound—I'm bound to thank you for it
Oh, I want to thank you for so many gifts
You gave me love and tenderness
I want to thank you
I want to thank you for your generosity,
The love, and the honesty that you gave to me
I want to thank you, show my gratitude,
My love and my respect for you
I want to thank you

The Dwelling Place

I had drawn a line emotionally. On one side was the day-to-day life that we lived. On the other side was the place I had come to name the Dwelling Place. It was a place that I could fall into head first and remain for hours—with energy drained and pools of tears overflowing from my eyes. Images of my beautiful boy in his last two weeks haunted me.

Picking up the pieces, moving on, and just living your life after a losing a child is a full-time job. It's like an inner dance, done amid the noise and bustle of what appears to be normal life. No one knows the hidden turmoil that stirs like a tornado in your stomach. No one sees how hard you push to not fall into the Dwelling Place—to remain out in the functioning world.

I had so many questions about the Dwelling Place. How long was it usual to stay there? It seemed like most of the people around me had resumed normalcy, so I fought the urge to dwell. But sometimes, it called to me. Sometimes I didn't want to fight it. So, I went there to dwell on what was, what could have been. I dwelled on the way that he died—that it was not from the cancer, but from complications from sepsis. I dwelled on what my child looked like at the end, how unfair and how cruel for such a beautiful soul to have to surrender to such a senseless way of dying.

The Dwelling Place had, and still has, a purpose. Being in touch with those feeling does matter. But mostly, I tried to think of Nick and seriously tried, I mean really, really tried, to imagine his journey. He surely had a dwelling place of his own, and he surely fought like hell to not go there.

And it worked for him.

He managed to function incredibly well, never dwelling on the awful reality that he faced every minute of his life.

Can I be half the person Nick was in the long run? I tried (and still try) as hard as I could. My friends and family have served as ropes that I hold on to, so I don't fall too far into my dwelling place. And it works…most of the time.

I had a bracelet designed with the letters *LLND*. His friends and our family wore them to remind us each to Live Like Nick Did. Those bracelets are a reminder to not take life for granted, ever. *It reminds me to not dwell on things I cannot change…and to change everything I can.*

Every day those words remind me to be as alive as I can be.

Rise like the Sun

Month after month went by without Nick, and life felt surreal. Days came and went and we often forgot what day it was. The structure of our lives had been completely dictated by "medical" days for so long that the transition back to living meaningful, mindful days with another purpose was difficult. But we continued to push forward. We established a memorial scholarship at Lynchburg College, and I continued to serve as president of Band of Parents.

I felt more attuned to the rhythms of nature. Steamy days, storm clouds in the afternoon, moonlit nights—these were, and still are, often my moments of feeling closest to Nick. The hardest part was always waking up in the morning. There was an anxiousness in crossing over from the peace of sleep to a new day—a day without my son. But every morning the sun kept on rising, kept offering a new day. And while sometimes, when the sun rose, I wanted to hide from the brightness and cover my heart with quiet darkness; on other days, the sun reminded me that the predictability of a new dawn brought comfort and hope that the day ahead would bring some glimmer of peace, and new memories to build upon.

Nick always rose like the sun. Even after the darkest of nights, filled with pain and exhaustion, he would rise with a smile and try and find the moments to build memories and good days.

Now, each morning as I rose with the sun, I listened to the birds and appreciated the coolness of the morning, and I felt overwhelming gratitude for the love expressed by all of the people in my life. Those people were and are as constant as the sun—that always rises.

Fourth of July

Another in a series of "firsts," as the year sped by, was the Fourth of July, 2011. We went to the town parade, the one Nick was a part of so many times, with his go-kart, his big wheel, his bicycle, his roller blades. We remembered pie eating contests, egg toss challenges, swinging high on the swings. I watched the festivities with memories flooding my heart.

We weren't martyrs. We did not want to isolate and "dwell" too much. We wanted to join the living. *We pushed ourselves to show up, to engage, to reconnect with events and friends.*

Through it all, my sweet Nick seemed to be everywhere.

And yet, he was nowhere.

After the pot luck dinner and the egg toss and the communion with friends, we went to be with him at the grave. At the cemetery, we walked up the hill from our car with Nick's dog Bailey. We put down a blanket and spent some time in silence. Kelliann had been there, and left a white, wooden star in the ground with her kisses on it. Alyson had been there too. We didn't know, but later, she posted a picture of herself on Facebook, looking up at the sky from the same spot we spread our blanket.

Looking up, we didn't see fireworks, but we saw the beautiful blue sky, and I wondered where Nick really was. It's an age-old question, and of course I know what all the responses usually are. But it is still a lonely place for a mother and father, to not be able to fully visualize where their child is.

Not in this lifetime, not in this human shape.

We sat by his grave and looked out at the multitude of flags that others had placed for their loved ones. We knew our pain was shared by all of humanity. The little flags each represented a life lost and a remembrance of a loved one.

It is part of being human, and it hurts.

We spent some time sitting on a blanket under the beech trees, talking about Camp Varsity and the passion Nick had for it. He always wanted to be there on the Fourth of July when he was a counselor. We wondered if Nick's camp family was thinking of him as they set off fireworks on the dam.

We felt sure they were.

Then we left. We went back to our house, we geared up for another day, we continued to do what we did and live on, trying so hard to Live Like Nick Did.

Courage-Strength-Family-Friends-Faith

September, 2011—The First Band of Parents Trial

Four months after the day we lost Nick, September arrived. Everyone around us was moving back into the familiar routine that fall and a new school year brings. At the same time, many of my friends were still living their routine of battle, living their lives around scans and treatments and moving from one stressful moment to the next.

We were just trying to move into a routine. Any routine.

As we fought to find our new path in life, we received bittersweet news. The antibody that was now fully funded by Band of Parents made it to the clinic in New York. The first two children started the trial. Here is the letter we received from Dr. Cheung:

Dear BOP:

As you have probably heard, we finally got the green light from the FDA. The first ever humanized form of antibody 3F8 is going to be given to neuroblastoma patients starting this week, having gone through all the hurdles, many unforeseen. I want to thank you all for this unprecedented grass root idea, your tireless effort and generosity, and above all, your faith in our ability to get this done. Our hu3F8 is one of the very few drugs specifically made for treating neuroblastoma patients in the history of medicine. We are proud of this enormous effort which will not be possible without your partnership. Words cannot describe the excitement of our clinical and research teams, and hope you will pray for its success, as we all do.

Sincerely,

nkc

The Story of the Red-Winged Blackbird

Several days after the service celebrating Nick's life, Jim and I decided to play golf. Nick would not have sat around thinking about maybe playing some golf—he would have *done* something to snap out of it and so would we!

Twice on the golf course, this little, red-winged blackbird showed up beside me. Once I was getting ready to tee off, and it just sat there, not flying away. Seven holes later, Jim and I were both close together again and the red-winged blackbird landed in the fairway not ten feet from us, and just stared. This bird's presence felt intentional.

Two weeks later, Jim went on his annual golf trip to Myrtle Beach. He was on a hole near a beautiful marsh with oyster shells lining the bank. He hit his shot just barely onto the green; then putted the ball to about four feet from the hole. As he was walking to the ball and lining up his next putt, a bird suddenly flapped and fluttered right above his head.

Jim looked up. It was a red-winged blackbird.

The bird refused to leave the green until Jim did. As he got to his golf cart, Jim burst into tears. It took him a couple of holes to recover, as the feeling was so intense.

In August, Jim and I took a trip out west, hoping it would help us heal. We spent a day rafting on the Colorado River and shared the story of the red-winged blackbird with our river guide, Nick's cousin Greg. Greg told us that he had never seen a red-winged blackbird. Well, as we pulled the raft out of the water to load it up, a red-winged blackbird swooped right by Greg's head.

I said, "Now you have!" Our other river guide, who lives in Colorado, said that he had never seen a red-winged blackbird on the river before.

Later, on that same trip, we had a profound experience that I had to write about it in a blog I kept.. which was also my way of connecting with Nick:

Before we left Santa Fe, we decided to pop into a couple of galleries. There are literally dozens and dozens on Canyon Road. We were drawn to one and walked in. There on the wall was a gorgeous oil canvas of a red-winged blackbird, maybe 3 feet by 3 feet, price. . .$2,700.00. If I could have I would have pulled it off the wall right then and purchased it. You are so amazing how you weave into our lives. What are the odds of choosing that gallery, among the many we could have walked into? What are the odds that the first painting was a single red-winged blackbird on a branch, with the title The Sentinel. . .meaning "watching guard over us?"

We left Santa Fe in awe of your spirit radiating inside of us, whispering through the red-winged blackbird, "I am here."

You never know who reads your blog. Shortly after returning from our trip, a total stranger contacted me. She had read my blog entry about the painting and wanted to purchase it for us. I was in shock. I told her we could never accept such a gift, but she insisted. She said she had a nice life, was financially comfortable, and had healthy children. She wanted to feel a part of something that had meaning. Finally, after much convincing, she got me to say yes to her generous gift.

We were able to track down the gallery, and the painting was sent to us. A true demonstration of love and friendship had come from a stranger.

Over the years, we have had other red-winged blackbird experiences. One that is etched on my heart is a family blessing. We were all gathered on our back porch with the sliding glass doors open in early spring. As we held hands as a family, just before the prayer began, the trill of a red-winged blackbird resounded through the room. We looked out, and there he was, sitting on the bird feeder, ushering in our prayer.

And so it is.

Faith is challenged, questioned, and interpreted many different ways. For us, knowing there is a spiritual realm after the earthly body is gone is an absolute. We all will face that part of our existence. Some will face it in an instant, some over years of suffering. Spirit dwells in each of us, and for us, Nick's spirit is demonstrated brightly through the wings of a bird, and for this I am so grateful.

Of course, not everyone receives this kind of sign. While we have been blessed in this regard and it is comforting, it doesn't change the reality. When the great divide between human flesh and spiritual essence occurs, it takes time, it takes patience, and it takes digging to your core to come up for air.

There is still air. There is still sunshine. There is still life in our humaneness. The challenges of illness and sudden loss will continue. It is how we draw on our resiliency, how we choose to navigate the compass points of our journey that makes the difference.

For us it has not been easy, and six years later, we continue to heal. At first we discovered that joy could creep back in, laughter could echo, and sleep could once again be deep and peaceful. The lessons from my son's tattoo are universal. They are the essence of humanity. Courage, Strength, Friendship, Family, Faith. In whatever shape or form you find them, build on these values in the good times. You may rely on them when life changes, and you need these compass points to lead you back.

Epilogue

Five Years Later

I boarded the Northeast Regional, heading back to New York City. It was almost eleven years to the day from our first terrifying journey into the unknown. But this trip had a happier purpose—to celebrate the success of Band of Parents, the foundation I helped form, at a rooftop fundraiser on a summer night.

Still, I was a parent who lost her child to the battle, so I went with a multitude of mixed emotions. The breakthrough treatment we championed came too late for Nick. I celebrated the success and pushed through the undercurrent of sadness. I was there to offer hope and support to those who were in the fight. That remains one of my ways to honor Nick.

I thought back to a conversation we had with Nick, back at the beginning of our ordeal, just after we met with the doctors the first time. I optimistically told him we had hope, because in older children, neuroblastoma could eventually be managed as a chronic disease. I told him he could very possibly live a long time like that. He looked at us and just said, "Did you really think I was going to die from this? I am not going to die."

Those words echoed in my brain throughout Nick's six-year battle. To the very end, he kept faith that there would be another step. The words of his tattoo inked on my skin and vibrating through my soul remind me every day how to navigate life, even when the unthinkable happens.

Those words and our story are the legacy and gift that my son leaves for you.

Thoughts and Poems

Expressing emotion through any art form can help heal. Music, art, writing—these are tools to ease the stress and pain… my way was these poems.

Your Angel Appeared…

Two souls wandering found each other's eyes
Tenderness, compassion, and love poured out
Hearts connected, and love was born
Each soul harbored pain and suffering, held in silence as their love grew
The safety of each other's arms melted any worry stirring inside
Time wasn't kind, and dark realities appeared—
A new world was born, with survival as the pulse of each new day
Wounds of your own hid deep inside
As your light radiated healing and comfort
Things born of spirit never die
But flesh and blood have to let go
Joined together for a common purpose
To shelter each other for a while
Shelter from past wounds, from realities whose burden was much to bear.
Remember what was created, what nourished and fed your broken soul

Use it to grow, use it to become
More than you ever could have been
Before your angel appeared
Letting go, but living on with the lessons born of a love never forgotten

One Tear Away

Just in case you are wondering, how to say what you say
Try to remember, for us, each day—
we are all just one tear away
One tear away from losing
the composure we struggle to keep
One tear away from dropping the mask
That keeps us from the constant urge to weep
Who we were we aren't right now
It's really hard to explain,
All we ask from those who care
is to be patient, and accept our pain
Our emotional armor causes us to be more tense
to not have a lot to give
It takes all we have to do what we do
Helping our children live.
So, if you see us close up
Or from afar
If you don't know what to say
Remember, your words can lift us or drop us
Because we are always just one tear away.

From Jeff Franca- written the morning of Nick's passing

For My Brother
On this morning the birds sing the most beautiful song
Leaves and flowers shine brightly
Another brother blesses the earth, the heavens, his loved ones
His struggle vanishes and his spirit erupts
An energy awakes in the souls he has touched
An eternal connection of love and strength
Strength that is now passed on and love that unites us all
The joy of being and Angel rewards his sacrifice
He believes in us
He loves us,
He is there for us
This is the morning of new light
A light that now shines brighter than ever
His spirit is the fuel
Love the light
These are his gifts

Acknowledgments

To all the voices that whispered to me over the years, "You have to write a book," thank you. I had many doubts and many fears. A worldwide audience kept encouraging me, which ended up giving me the drive to finish the book. I want to thank my editor, Lisa Canfield, for helping me shape my journal into a story. I want to thank my husband, who would rather "close the door." Instead, he encouraged and supported me to keep Nick's story alive, as it would support and encourage others. I want to thank him for having the courage to read the final manuscript and offer small changes, as he read it with strength and courage, guided by the tattoo. Most of all, I want to thank the reader of this book. The perspective gained through my son's journey has universal themes that offer hope and encouragement. Walk with courage. Walk with strength. Find faith in something. Lean on friends and family. If you gain just a glimmer of that perspective, then my goal is met, and my son's legacy lives on, in you. Thank you.

> What is it to die but to stand naked in the wind and to melt into the sun?
> And what is it to cease breathing, but to free the breath from its restless tides, that it may rise and expand and seek God unencumbered?
> Only when you drink from the river of silence shall you indeed sing.
> And when you have reached the mountain top, then you shall begin to climb.
> And when the earth shall claim your limbs, then shall you truly dance.
>
> —Kahlil Gibran

About the Author

Caryn Franca maintained personal journals and a blog throughout her son's six-year battle with cancer. She is the cofounder and former president of Band of Parents, a nonprofit that raises money to fund research for less toxic treatments for the childhood cancer neuroblastoma. Caryn remains on the board of Band of Parents. To date the group has raised $6 million and has funded a trial that is now standard protocol at Memorial Sloan Kettering Cancer Center in New York. More information about the nonprofit can be found at bandofparents.org.

After earning a Bachelor's Degree, Caryn started her career as an elementary school teacher. For the past twenty three years she has built and maintained a flexible career as a wellness coach with Shaklee Corporation. Caryn also was trained as a life coach and had a private practice until her son was diagnosed. Caryn loves life, fun, friends, family, golf, travel, and making a difference. This is her first book.

Made in the USA
Middletown, DE
20 August 2017